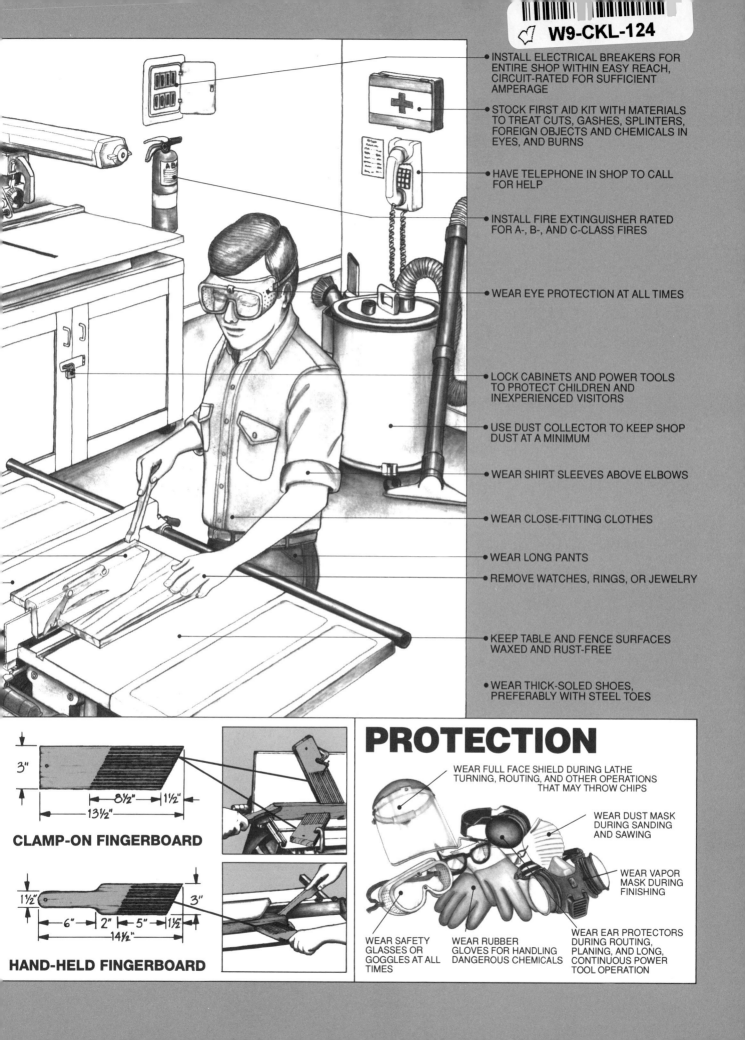

- INSTALL ELECTRICAL BREAKERS FOR ENTIRE SHOP WITHIN EASY REACH, CIRCUIT-RATED FOR SUFFICIENT AMPERAGE
- STOCK FIRST AID KIT WITH MATERIALS TO TREAT CUTS, GASHES, SPLINTERS, FOREIGN OBJECTS AND CHEMICALS IN EYES, AND BURNS
- HAVE TELEPHONE IN SHOP TO CALL FOR HELP
- INSTALL FIRE EXTINGUISHER RATED FOR A-, B-, AND C-CLASS FIRES
- WEAR EYE PROTECTION AT ALL TIMES
- LOCK CABINETS AND POWER TOOLS TO PROTECT CHILDREN AND INEXPERIENCED VISITORS
- USE DUST COLLECTOR TO KEEP SHOP DUST AT A MINIMUM
- WEAR SHIRT SLEEVES ABOVE ELBOWS
- WEAR CLOSE-FITTING CLOTHES
- WEAR LONG PANTS
- REMOVE WATCHES, RINGS, OR JEWELRY
- KEEP TABLE AND FENCE SURFACES WAXED AND RUST-FREE
- WEAR THICK-SOLED SHOES, PREFERABLY WITH STEEL TOES

CLAMP-ON FINGERBOARD

3"
8½" 1½"
13½"

HAND-HELD FINGERBOARD

1½"
3"
6" 2" 5" 1½"
14½"

PROTECTION

WEAR FULL FACE SHIELD DURING LATHE TURNING, ROUTING, AND OTHER OPERATIONS THAT MAY THROW CHIPS

WEAR DUST MASK DURING SANDING AND SAWING

WEAR VAPOR MASK DURING FINISHING

WEAR SAFETY GLASSES OR GOGGLES AT ALL TIMES

WEAR RUBBER GLOVES FOR HANDLING DANGEROUS CHEMICALS

WEAR EAR PROTECTORS DURING ROUTING, PLANING, AND LONG, CONTINUOUS POWER TOOL OPERATION

THE WORKSHOP COMPANION®

WOOD AND WOODWORKING MATERIALS

TECHNIQUES FOR BETTER WOODWORKING

by Nick Engler

Rodale Press
Emmaus, Pennsylvania

Printed in the United States of America on acid-free ⊗, recycled ✿ paper

If you have any questions or comments concerning this book, please write:
    Rodale Press
    Book Readers' Service
    33 East Minor Street
    Emmaus, PA 18098

About the Author: Nick Engler is an experienced wood-worker, writer, teacher, and inventor. He worked as a luthier for many years, making traditional American musi-cal instruments before he founded *Hands On!* magazine. He has taught at the University of Cincinnati and gives wood-working seminars around the country. He contributes to woodworking magazines and designs tools for America's Best Tool Company. This is his forty-fourth book.

Series Editor: Kevin Ireland
Editors: Ken Burton
            Roger Yepsen
Copy Editor: Sarah Dunn
Graphic Designer: Linda Watts
Illustrators: Mary Jane Favorite
            David Van Etten
Master Craftsman: Jim McCann
Photographer: Karen Callahan
Cover Photographer: Mitch Mandel
Proofreader: Hue Park
Indexer: Beverly Bremer
Interior and endpaper illustrations by Mary Jane Favorite
Produced by Bookworks, Inc., West Milton, Ohio

Library of Congress Cataloging-in-Publication Data

Engler, Nick.
    Wood and woodworking materials: techniques for
    better woodworking / by Nick Engler
        p.   cm. — (The Workshop companion)
    Includes index.
    ISBN 0–87596–722–1 (hardcover : alk. paper)
    1. Woodwork. 2. Wood. I. Title.
    II. Series: Engler, Nick. Workshop companion.
TT180.E66   1995
684'.08 — dc20   95–39658

Special Thanks to:

Jon Arno
Durst Lumber Company
Berkley, Michigan

Better Built Corporation
Wilmington, Massachusetts

Forest Products Laboratory
Madison, Wisconsin

Georgia-Pacific Corporation
Atlanta, Georgia

Sam and Wendy Marcum
Kettering, Ohio

Rod Miller
Miller Logging and Lumber Sales
West Manchester, Ohio

Mark Miller
Frank Miller Lumber Company
Union City, Indiana

North American Plywood Corporation
Jersey City, New Jersey

Paxton Beautiful Woods
Cincinnati, Ohio

Pierson-Hollowell Company
Lawrenceburg, Indiana

Israel Sack, Inc.
New York, New York

Wertz Hardware
West Milton, Ohio

Wood-Mizer Products, Inc.
Indianapolis, Indiana

The Workshops of David T. Smith
Morrow, Ohio

Photo on lower left page 4 from *Identifying Wood* by R. Bruce Hoadley. Used with permission of The Taunton Press, Inc., 63 South Main Street, P.O. Box 5506, Newtown, CT 06470. ©1990 The Taunton Press, Inc. All rights reserved.

CONTENTS

TECHNIQUES

iii

PROJECTS

TECHNIQUES

1

THE NATURE OF WOOD

Wood is the most widely used building material on the planet, and for good reason. It's easy to work, attractive, abundant, relatively inexpensive, and its sources are renewable. Pound for pound, it's stronger than steel. Properly cared for, it will last indefinitely. And there are few limits to its versatility. You can use it to build anything from a tiny box to a huge barn. It can be made into dozens of useful materials, including plywood, particleboard, plastic laminates, paper, turpentine, and cellulose film, just to name a few.

Wood is also one of the most complex building materials. Metals and plastics are *isotropic;* that is, their properties are consistent throughout, in any direction. But wood is *orthotropic*. Its strength is different along the grain than across it. It expands and contracts more in one direction than another. Not even its color is consistent. Wood from the interior of the tree is often much darker than wood closer to the surface.

To work with wood — and have it work for you — you must know something of its complex nature. In particular, you should realize that it has three unique properties that affect the quality of everything you build. These are *grain, movement,* and *strength*.

WOOD GRAIN

HOW WOOD GROWS

To best understand wood grain, it helps to know how it develops. A tree grows in concentric layers, which reveal themselves when you slice the trunk horizontally. At the very center of the trunk is the *pith*. In some trees, this may be much softer or a different color than the surrounding *heartwood*. Heartwood is dead cells that no longer serve any purpose other than to support the tree. Next is the *sapwood,* which carries the sap (water, minerals, and plant sugars) between the roots and the crown. This is usually lighter in color than the heartwood. Outside the sapwood, close to the surface, is a thin layer of living, growing cells called the *cambium*. These cells manufacture the wood. The cambium is covered by a protective layer of *bark*. (*SEE FIGURE 1-1.*)

FOR YOUR INFORMATION

Typically, the heartwood has the best color and is preferred for fine woodworking. But this is not always the case. In a few species, particularly maple and other light-colored woods, the sapwood is preferred for its consistent creamy white color.

The cambium expands a little each year. In the spring, it grows rapidly, creating light-colored *spring-wood*. It begins to slow down in the summer, producing darker *summerwood*. The summerwood is also somewhat denser and harder than the springwood. In the winter, the cambium becomes dormant and does not grow at all until the next spring. This growing cycle creates *growth rings*. (*SEE FIGURE 1-2.*)

1-1 There are three major parts to a living tree — the *root system* (1), the *trunk* (2), and the *crown* (3). Most lumber comes from the trunk, although all the woody parts can be used to make particleboard and other products. These woody parts grow in concentric layers. At the center of a trunk is the *pith* (4). Surrounding this are the *heartwood* (5) and the *sapwood* (6). Close to the surface is the *cambium* (7), which manufactures wood cells as it grows outward. The cambium is protected by the *bark* (8).

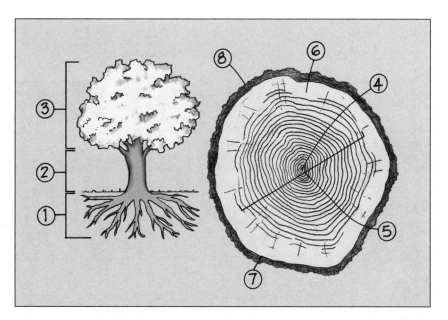

1-2 The cambium grows very rapidly in the spring, producing light-colored *springwood* (1). It slows down in the summer, producing darker *summerwood* (2), then goes dormant in the winter. This growing cycle produces the characteristic *growth rings* or *annual rings* in wood.

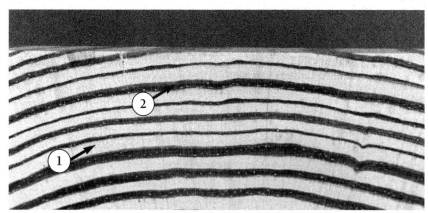

As it grows, the cambium generates two types of wood cells. Most of these are long, narrow *longitudinal cells* that grow parallel to the length of the root, trunk, or limb. The cambium also makes a smaller number of *ray cells* that align themselves in strings (called *rays*) extending out from the pith, perpendicular to the length. (*SEE FIGURE 1-3.*)

As the cambium grows outward, the living protoplasm inside the cells dies and decays, leaving behind the cell walls. The walls are composed mostly of *cellulose* and they are bound together with a gluelike substance called *lignin*. The hollow longitudinal cells, now part of the sapwood, conduct the sap up and down the tree. The hollow rays often store plant sugars.

After several growing cycles, the sapwood turns to heartwood. As it does this, the sap dries up and chemical compounds called *extractives* form on the cell walls. These give a wood its characteristic color. Extractives also affect the stability, strength, and hard-

ness of the wood. They sometimes contain minerals that dull cutting tools, or toxins that help protect the wood from fungi and bacteria.

TYPES OF GRAIN

Because of the way in which wood grows, every board has a distinct structure or *grain*. It also has a definite *grain direction*, parallel to the longitudinal cells. The grain appears differently depending on how you cut the wood in relation to the grain direction and its growth rings (*SEE FIGURE 1-4*).

■ When you cut wood across the grain (perpendicular to the grain direction and the concentric growth rings) you see the *end grain*. This commonly appears at the ends of a board.

■ Cut the wood parallel to the grain direction and tangent to the growth rings, and you'll reveal *flat grain* (also called *tangential grain* or *plain grain*).

■ Cut it parallel to the grain direction but through the radius of the growth rings, and you'll see *quarter grain* (also called *radial grain*).

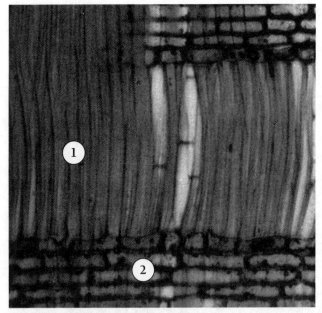

1-3 This small piece of red oak, magnified 75 times, reveals a complex structure. Most of the wood is made up of long, narrow *longitudinal cells* (1) growing roughly parallel to one another. There are also a few *ray cells* arranged in strings or *rays* (2) extending out from the center of the tree, roughly perpendicular to the longitudinal cells. Both contribute to the characteristic appearance of the wood grain.

1-4 The wood grain appears differ-ently depending on how you slice the wood. Cut it perpendicular to the grain direction to see the *end grain* (1). Cut it parallel to the grain direction and tangent to the growth rings to show *flat grain* (2). Or, cut it parallel to the grain direction and through the radius of the growth rings to show the *quarter grain* (3). On each surface of a board, one type of grain usually predominates.

There are several ways for a sawyer to cut up a tree trunk, and each shows different grain patterns on faces and edges of the boards. The most common method is to *plain saw,* or "saw around" a log. Plain-sawn boards show flat grain on the face and quarter grain on the edges. *(See Figure 1-5.)* The sawyer can also *quarter saw* a trunk, splitting it into quarters and cutting the quarters into boards. Quarter-sawn boards show quarter grain on the faces and flat grain on the

edges. *(See Figure 1-6.)* Or, he can *live saw* the trunk, sawing through the diameter. (This is sometimes called *sawing through-and-through.*) Live sawing produces wide boards with mixed grain. *(See Figure 1-7.)*

Note: In many lumber mills, a board is considered to be quarter-sawn if the annual rings are between 90 and 45 degrees to its faces. If the angle is less than 45 degrees, the board is classified as plain-sawn. However, other mills make a finer distinction — if the

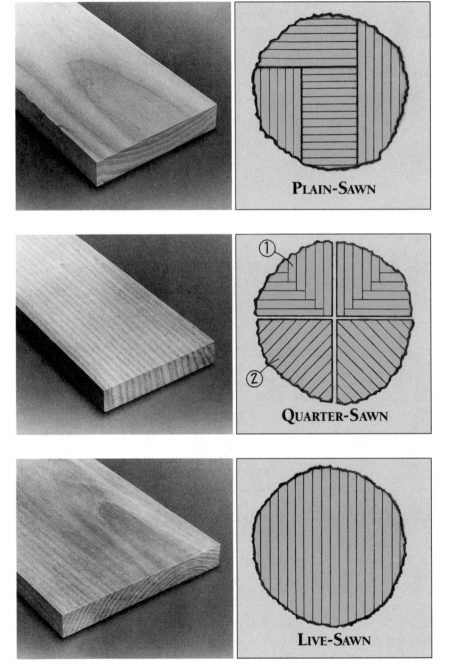

1-5 To *plain saw* a tree trunk, the sawyer saws several boards from one side, turns the trunk 90 degrees and saws several more, turns it another 90 degrees and continues in the same manner, "sawing around" the log. The resulting lumber shows flat grain on the face and quarter grain on the edges. This method produces the highest percentage of usable lumber from the tree, and consequently is the most common.

PLAIN-SAWN

1-6 To *quarter saw* a trunk, the sawyer first splits the log into quarters. Then he slices each quarter into boards, either by cutting the flat sides alternately (1) or sawing it through (2). On quarter-sawn boards, the quarter grain shows on the face and the flat grain on the edges.

QUARTER-SAWN

1-7 To *live saw* a trunk, the sawyer slices the log through the diameter without turning it. This produces much wider boards than other methods. The boards cut from the middle of the log show quarter grain on their faces; those cut near the surfaces show flat grain. Most boards, however, show *mixed grain* — flat grain near the center of the face and quarter grain closer to the edges.

LIVE-SAWN

rings are 90 to 60 degrees from the faces, it's quarter-sawn; 60 to 30 degrees is *rift-sawn,* and 30 to 0 degrees is plain-sawn. Using these classifications, standard quarter-sawing methods produce both quarter-sawn and rift-sawn lumber. (*SEE FIGURE 1-8.*)

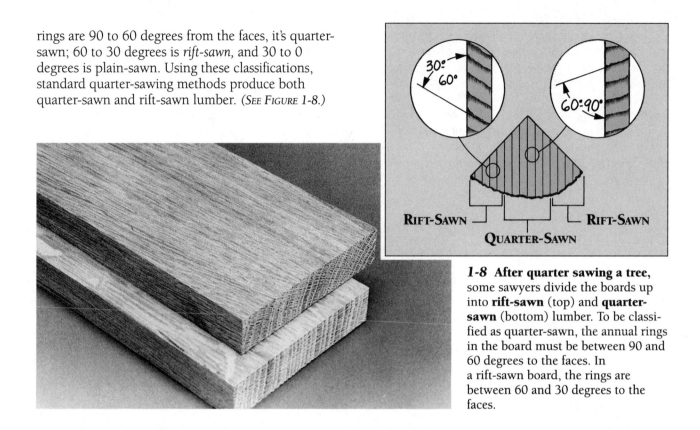

1-8 After quarter sawing a tree, some sawyers divide the boards up into **rift-sawn** (top) and **quarter-sawn** (bottom) lumber. To be classified as quarter-sawn, the annual rings in the board must be between 90 and 60 degrees to the faces. In a rift-sawn board, the rings are between 60 and 30 degrees to the faces.

For Your Information

Occasionally, the wood is sawed at an angle to the grain direction, like the ash board shown here, and shows *bastard grain* — somewhere in between

end grain, flat grain, and quarter grain. This often happens when the tree trunk is curved, as shown in the drawing.

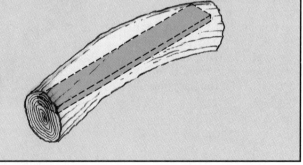

WOOD FIGURE

When a board has an unusual grain pattern, craftsmen say the wood has *figured grain.* There are several distinct types of wood figure (*SEE FIGURE 1-9*).

■ Quarter grain often shows *ray fleck* — stripes of color perpendicular to the grain, caused by the rays. When the rays are particularly large, as they are in oak, this is sometimes referred to as *silver grain.*

■ Where the trunk divides into smaller branches at

a crotch, the longitudinal cells grow in several directions. This produces a distinctive *crotch figure.*

■ In some wood species the longitudinal cells, instead of growing in parallel lines, arrange themselves in parallel waves. This produces *curly grain.*

■ Occasionally, a fungus causes small round dimples to develop in the layers of longitudinal cells, creating *bird's-eyes.*

■ Larger dimples, arranged close together, produce a *quilted figure*. These, too, are thought to be the result of a fungus that affects the longitudinal cell growth.

■ In a few species, such as mahogany, the longitudinal cells don't grow precisely parallel to the trunk, but spiral around it. When these woods are quarter-sawn or cut through the radius of the trunk, they show a *ribbon figure*.

■ Now and then, large bulges known as *burls* develop on the sides of trees. Inside these bulges, the longitudinal cells swirl around aimlessly, producing a distinctive *burl figure*.

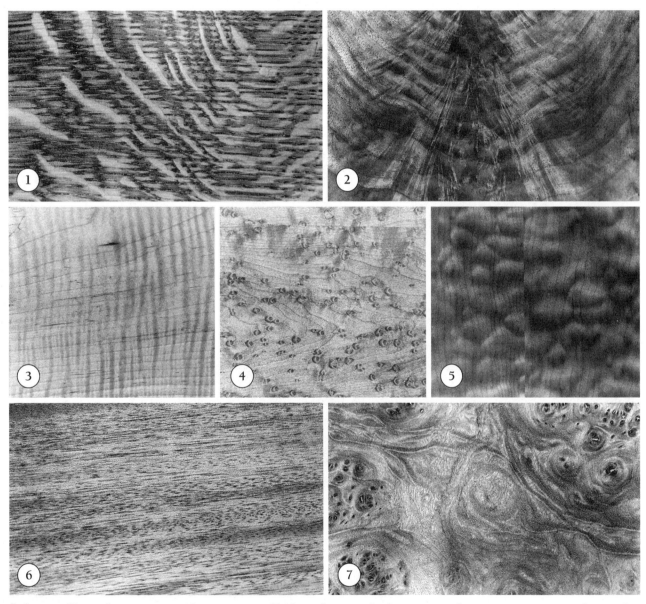

1-9 Not all wood grain is straight and even. Sometimes the longitudinal cells and the rays grow in unusual patterns, known as *figured grain*. For example, the large rays in white oak produce *silver grain* (1). *Crotch figure* (2) is cut from the crotch of a walnut tree, where the trunk divides into smaller branches. Maple shows several different types of figure — *curly grain* (3) occurs when the longitudinal maple cells grow in waves; *bird's-eyes* (4) are caused by small dimples in the cell layers; and *quilted figure* (5) is the result of larger dimples. The longitudinal cells of mahogany sometimes spiral around a trunk, creating a distinct *ribbon figure* (6). And any wood species may produce large growths or burls. When cut or sliced, these display a swirling *burl figure* (7).

KNOTS AND OTHER DEFECTS

Not all anomalies in the wood grain produce an attractive figure. Some detract from the appearance or weaken the structure of the wood. Most craftsmen try to avoid these common *defects* (SEE FIGURE 1-10).

■ *Knots* occur wherever the trunk shoots out smaller branches. As the tree grows, both the trunk and the branch get bigger, and a cone-shaped area of branch wood develops within the trunk. Inside this branch wood, the grain takes off in a different direction from the surrounding grain in the trunk. This appears as a knot in the sawed lumber. (SEE FIGURES *1-11* AND *1-12*.)

■ *Reaction wood* forms when a tree grows at an angle to the pull of gravity. The tree may be growing on a steep slope, have become partially uprooted or starved for sunlight, or bent under the weight of snow and ice. When this happens, the tree reacts by buttressing itself to provide additional support. Wood that grows under these circumstances is harder and more brittle than normal wood, and it has internal tensions that cause it to bend or bow when cut.

■ *Molds, fungi, and bacteria* growing in the wood may ruin its appearance or structure. Some of these cause decay or *wood rot*; others discolor the wood. *Blue stain* is a common discoloration caused by mold.

■ *Insects* may also damage the wood. Fly larvae can cause *pith flecks*. Powder-post beetles, carpenter ants, and termites can leave *bore holes*.

■ When wood is improperly dried or under continual stress, the fibers separate, creating *checks, splits,* and *shakes*. For example, when the ends dry and shrink before the rest of the board, *end checks* develop. If the tree has been bent by wind, ice, or snow, the annual rings may separate and the lumber will be plagued by *wind shakes*.

FOR YOUR INFORMATION

A *check* is a crack that does not go all the way through a board, while a *split* does. Both are roughly perpendicular to the growth rings. When a crack follows a ring, it is known as a *shake*.

1-10 **Defects detract from the** appearance of the wood and may affect its structural integrity. For example, a *knot* (1) not only interrupts the grain pattern, it weakens the wood in the vicinity. *Reaction wood* (2) has internal stresses that cause it to warp, bow, or twist. Molds and microbes may *stain* (3) a board or cause it to rot away. Insects eat *bore holes* (4) through wood. If the wood is stressed or improperly dried, it may develop *checks* (5) and other sorts of cracks.

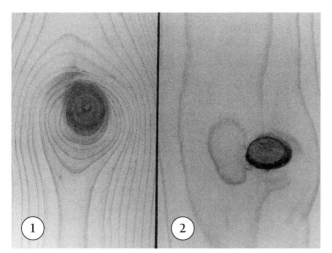

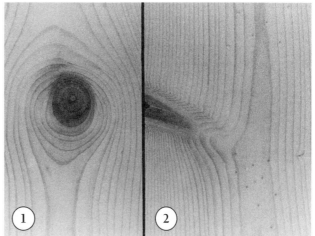

1-11 Wherever a trunk divides
into smaller limbs, it creates a *knot*. If
the limb is living and growing at the
time the tree is harvested, it will form
an intergrown or *tight knot* (1).
When the tree is sawn into boards,
the tight knots appear as a continuous part of the surrounding wood.
If you're going to work with knotty
lumber, this is the most desirable
type. If, however, the limb dies and
the tree grows around it, the dead
stump will show up as a *loose knot*
(2). Loose knots often drop out of
the wood, leaving knot holes.

1-12 Knots differ in appearance
depending on how they are sliced. If
they are sawed tangentially (tangent
to the growth rings of the trunk and
perpendicular to the branch), they
become *round knots* (1). When
sawed radially (through the radius
of the growth rings and parallel to
the branch), they appear as *spike
knots* (2).

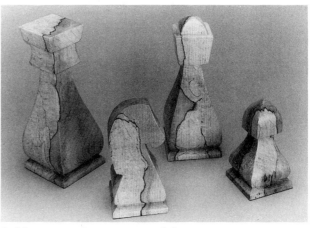

1-13 In specific instances, defects
can be desirable. These chess pieces
are made from *spalted maple* — wood
that has been stained by a fungus.
Ordinarily, craftsmen avoid stained
wood. But in this case, the spalting
gives the wood an exotic appearance
that adds visual interest to these
chess pieces. **Note:** Some craftsmen
intentionally spalt maple and birch
by leaving the logs laying in a wet,
shady area or tall grass for several
months before taking them to a
sawmill.

Other defects aren't quite so common. Some softwoods develop *pitch pockets* — cavities in the wood
that ooze sap. When boards are bundled and labeled
before shipping, the metal bands and printed labels
may leave stains. In walnut and cherry, the color difference between the heartwood and the sapwood is so
great that many craftsmen consider sapwood to be a
defect. In choosing wood, you have to be on the
lookout for any irregularities in the grain that may
detract from your project.

There are also some instances in which a specific
defect may be desirable. In "knotty pine" paneling, for
instance, the knots are considered attractive. White
rot fungus, if arrested in the early stages before the
wood decays, stains the wood grain with a marbled
pattern called *spalting*. Spalted wood makes striking
turnings and small projects. (*See Figure 1-13.*) And
powder-post beetles leave an appealing pattern of tiny
holes in wormy chestnut.

How Wood Grain Affects Design

It's the details that make the difference between a great piece of craftsmanship and a good effort. And one of the most commonly overlooked details is *wood grain.* The grain is a strong visual element that can either complement the design of a woodworking project or detract from it. Here are a few tricks to keep the wood grain working for you.

1 If the design is symmetrical, the wood grain should be symmetrical as well. The cabinet on the left has two different door panels, each showing a different grain pattern. As a result, the cabinet looks asymmetrical. The cabinet on the right has panels that were *book-matched* — resawn from the same board so they match almost precisely. This reinforces the symmetry.

2 Don't pay attention to just the panels and other broad expanses of wood when arranging the wood grain. The narrow rails and stiles will also have visual impact. The helter-skelter grain in the frame members on the left cabinet looks awful. The straight grain in the middle cabinet is a slight improvement, but it's unexciting. The carefully arranged curved grain in the right cabinet does interesting things for the design, almost making the front look bowed.

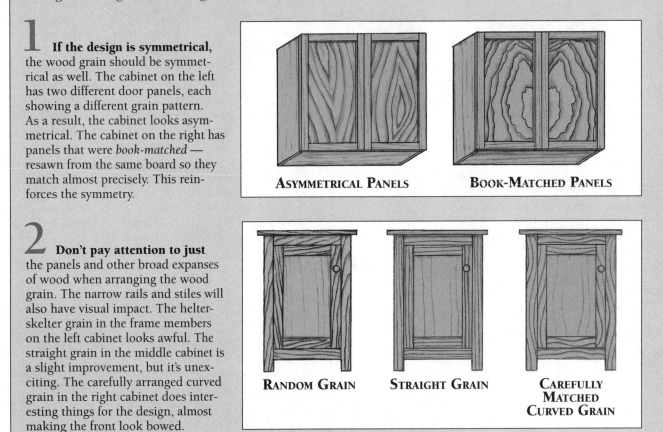

ASYMMETRICAL PANELS   **BOOK-MATCHED PANELS**

RANDOM GRAIN   **STRAIGHT GRAIN**   **CAREFULLY MATCHED CURVED GRAIN**

Wood Movement

Wood moves. If you work wood, this is extremely important to understand. Owing to its unique structure, wood is not a stable material; it's constantly expanding or contracting. And you must cope with this movement every time you build a project.

MOISTURE CONTENT AND RELATIVE HUMIDITY

Wood shrinks and swells as its *moisture content* changes. In freshly cut "green wood," liquid sap fills the cell cavities. This *free water* (as the sap is called) accounts for about 72 percent of the moisture in the wood, varying slightly from species to species. The remaining 28 percent saturates the fibers in the cell walls. The *bound water* in the fibers causes them to swell, the same way a sponge swells when you wet it. **Note:** Moisture content of 28 percent is called the *fiber saturation point,* at which point the wood fibers have absorbed as much water as they possibly can and are swollen as big as they're going to get.

As wood dries, it loses free water first, then bound water. It's fairly stable while the free water is evaporating, but once the moisture content drops below 28 percent — the fiber saturation point — it begins to lose bound water and the fibers shrink. The wood dries to an average moisture content between 4 and

3 **Wood grain can cause an** optical illusion, making a straight board appear to be curved or angled. This can work with the design or against it. All three of these tables have straight legs. The grain in the left table's legs slopes in, making it look unstable. The grain in the bottom table's legs is straight and uninteresting, while the grain in the right table's legs slopes out, making it appear solid and sturdy.

4 **When you must cut curves,** give some thought to how the growth rings will appear on the curved surfaces. On the left cabriole leg, the rings run diagonally from side to side, and the grain pattern fights with the leg's curves. In the middle leg, the rings run from face to face. The grain pattern appears uneven — compressed on one side and spread out on the other. On the right leg, the rings run diagonally from front to back, so the grain follows the curves of the legs.

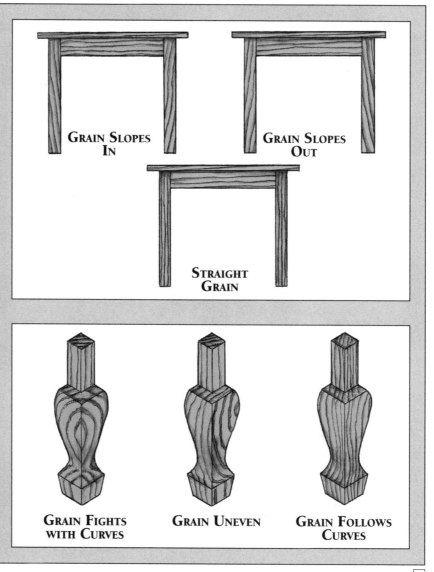

GRAIN SLOPES IN

GRAIN SLOPES OUT

STRAIGHT GRAIN

GRAIN FIGHTS WITH CURVES

GRAIN UNEVEN

GRAIN FOLLOWS CURVES

11 percent, depending on the area of the country you live in — *but it never really comes to rest!* The amount of bound water in the wood changes as the amount of moisture in the surrounding atmosphere varies, gaining or losing about 1 percent moisture content for every 5 percent change in the *relative humidity.* (SEE FIGURE 1-14.)

The wood swells as it absorbs moisture and shrinks as it releases it. And because the relative humidity usually increases in the summer and decreases in the winter, wood tends to expand in the summer and contract in the winter.

FOR YOUR INFORMATION

Relative humidity is the ratio of actual moisture (*absolute humidity*) in the atmosphere to the maximum amount of moisture it will hold at its present temperature. It's possible for the absolute humidity to change while the relative humidity stays the same. For instance, if both the absolute humidity and the temperature rise at the same time and at the proper rate, the relative humidity will remain constant. Wood won't move with changes in absolute humidity, only relative humidity.

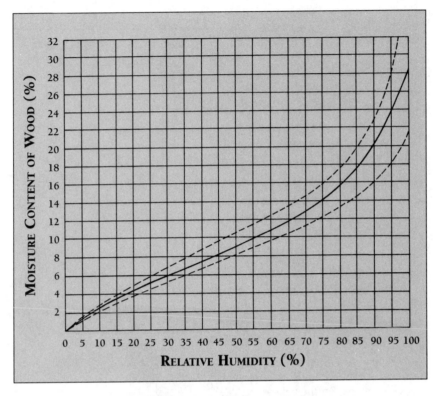

1-14 The moisture content of wood varies with the relative humidity of the surrounding air, as this chart shows. Different species absorb and release moisture at slightly different rates, but most fall within the dashed lines. Note that no matter how humid the weather becomes, the moisture content of the wood never rises much above 28 percent. This is the *fiber saturation point* — the point at which the wood fibers have absorbed as much *bound water* as they possibly can. For the moisture content to rise above that point, the cell cavities have to fill up with *free water*. And for this to happen, the wood has to be immersed in water.

DIRECTION OF MOVEMENT

Although it's in constant motion, wood does not move equally in all directions. This, too, is due to the wood structure. For practical purposes, wood is stable along the wood grain, expanding and contracting only about 0.1 percent. That means an 8-foot-long green board will only shrink about 1/16 inch as it dries. However, wood moves substantially *across* the grain. Furthermore, it moves almost twice as much *tangent* to the growth rings as it does radial to them — 8 percent versus 4 percent, on the average. (*SEE FIGURE 1-15.*) **Note:** Different species expand and contract different amounts. "Tangential and Radial Wood Movement" on page 14 lists the percentages for specific woods.

The difference in tangential and radial movement has some important consequences. Depending on how a board is sawed from a tree, it may *change shape* as it expands and contracts. Square stock becomes diamond shaped, round stock becomes oval. (*SEE FIGURE 1-16.*) Furthermore, some cutting methods produce more stable lumber than others. For example, a quarter-sawn board moves less and remains flatter than a plain-sawn board of the same size. (*SEE FIGURE 1-17.*) This is useful to know when you are selecting wood for various parts of a project.

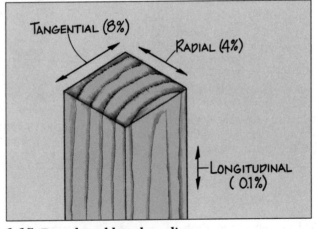

1-15 Every board has three dis-tinct planes, defined by the grain direction and the growth rings. The *longitudinal plane* is parallel to the wood grain. The *tangential plane* is perpendicular to the wood grain and tangent to the growth rings. The *radial plane* is perpendicular to the grain and extends out from the pith through the radius of the growth rings. Wood is fairly stable along the longitudinal plane, but (on the average) it expands and contracts 8 percent tangentially and 4 percent radially.

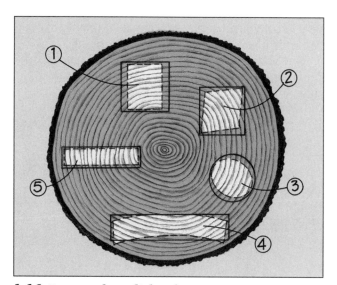

1-16 Because the radial and tan-
gential movement is uneven, boards
tend to change shape as they expand
and contract. The way in which they
change shape depends on how they
are cut from the tree. For example, if
the annual rings run from side to
side in a square table leg, the leg will
become rectangular as it shrinks (1).
If the rings run diagonally from
corner to corner, the leg will shrink
to a diamond shape (2). A round
dowel becomes an oval (3). A plain-
sawn board cups in the opposite
direction of the growth rings (4),
while a quarter-sawn board holds its
shape (5).

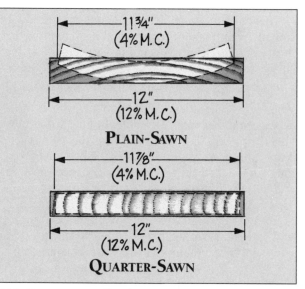

1-17 Quarter-sawn lumber is
more stable than plain-sawn. A
quarter-sawn board is cut radially.
Consequently, it expands and contracts across its width only half as
much as a tangentially cut plain-
sawn board. Additionally, plain-sawn
lumber tends to cup in the opposite
direction of the growth rings when
it shrinks. The outside face (the face
farthest from the center of the tree)
shrinks a little faster than the inside
face, causing uneven tension in the
board. This tension is eliminated
in quarter-sawn lumber and it
remains flat.

ESTIMATING WOOD MOVEMENT

It's not always enough to know that wood moves in
two directions. Often, you need to know *how much*
the wood moves. For example, when cutting a panel
to fit a frame, how large should the gap be between
the panel and the frame? If you make the gap too
small, the panel will expand and break the frame.
Make it too large, and the panel will fall out of the
frame when it shrinks. Miscalculations like these
cause doors and drawers to stick, tabletops to split
and buckle, and entire assemblies to fail.

There are a few simple rules of thumb to help you
estimate wood movement. First, look at the boards
and decide whether they show mostly flat grain or
quarter grain on the face. With boards showing flat
grain, allow for ¼ inch of *total* wood movement for
every 12 inches across the grain. With those showing
quarter grain, allow for ⅛ inch of movement. (The

difference is that flat-grain boards expand and contract *tangentially,* while those showing quarter grain
move *radially.*) This accommodates an annual fluctua-
tion of up to 8 percent in moisture content — much
more than is common in any part of the United States.

After figuring the total allowance for wood movement, consider the time of year. Wood shrinks to its
smallest dimension in the winter and swells to its maximum size in the summer. When building in the
winter, plan on the wood expanding the total
allowance. In the summer, plan on it shrinking the
same amount — but allow ¹⁄₁₆ inch for every 12 inches
across the grain for expansion, just in case. In the
spring and fall, split the allowance on the assumption
that the wood will expand half the total and shrink the
other half.

This method works for most situations, but occasionally you must figure the wood movement with a little more precision. When this is the case, use this simple formula

$$M = [(SMC - WMC) \div 0.28] \times TRM \times D$$

where M is the total wood movement, SMC is the average summer moisture content of the wood in the area the piece will be used, WMC is the average winter moisture content, TRM is the percentage of tangential or radial movement for the wood species, and D is the dimension across the grain.

Let's say you're making a table for a friend in St. Louis and you need to know how much a 30-inch-wide quarter-sawn white oak tabletop will expand and contract. First look up the radial movement percentage of white oak in "Tangential and Radial Wood Movement" on this page. It's 5.6 percent, or 0.056. Then consult "Average Indoor Moisture Content" on the opposite page to find that the average summer moisture content in St. Louis is about 10 percent (0.10) and drops to 7.5 percent (0.075) in the winter. Subtract the winter moisture content from the summer moisture content and divide by the maximum moisture content — 28 percent or 0.28. Multiply the result times the radial movement percentage (0.056) times the width of the tabletop (30 inches). This tells you to expect that the tabletop will expand and contract about .15 inch each year —

$$[(0.10 - 0.075) \div 0.28] \times 0.056 \times 30 = 0.15.$$

TANGENTIAL AND RADIAL WOOD MOVEMENT

These percentages indicate how much you can expect a green board to shrink across the grain when it releases *all* of its bound water (from 28 percent moisture content to completely dry).

SPECIES	% TANGENTIAL MOVEMENT	% RADIAL MOVEMENT	SPECIES	% TANGENTIAL MOVEMENT	% RADIAL MOVEMENT
Domestic Hardwoods			**Domestic Softwoods**		
Alder, Red	7.3	4.4	Cedar, Aromatic Red	5.2	3.3
Ash, White	7.8	4.9	Cedar, Western Red	5.0	2.4
Aspen (Cottonwood)	6.7	3.5	Cedar, White	4.9	2.2
Basswood	9.3	6.6	Cypress	6.2	3.8
Beech	11.9	5.5	Fir, Douglas	7.3	4.5
Birch, White	8.6	6.3	Hemlock	7.9	4.3
Birch, Yellow	8.1	3.6	Larch	9.1	4.5
Butternut	6.4	3.4	Pine, Ponderosa	6.2	3.9
Catalpa	4.9	2.5	Pine, Sugar	5.6	2.9
Cherry	7.1	3.7	Pine, White	7.4	4.1
Chestnut	6.7	3.4	Pine, Yellow	6.1	2.1
Elm	9.5	4.2	Redwood	4.9	2.2
Hickory, Shagbark	10.5	7.0	Spruce, Sitka	7.5	4.3
Holly	9.9	4.8	**Imported Woods**		
Maple, Hard	9.9	4.8	Bubinga	8.4	5.8
Maple, Soft	8.2	4.0	Ebony	6.5	5.5
Oak, Red	8.9	4.2	Lauan	8.0	3.8
Oak, White	10.5	5.6	Mahogany, African	4.5	2.5
Pecan	8.9	4.9	Mahogany, Genuine	4.1	3.0
Poplar, Yellow	8.2	4.6	Primavera	5.2	3.1
Sweetgum	10.2	5.3	Purpleheart	6.1	3.2
Sycamore	8.4	5.0	Rosewood, Brazilian	4.6	2.9
Walnut	7.8	5.5	Rosewood, Indian	5.8	2.7
Willow	8.7	3.3	Teak	5.8	2.5

AVERAGE INDOOR MOISTURE CONTENT

The moisture content of seasoned lumber changes as the relative humidity in its geographical area rises and falls. The top map shows the approximate average moisture content in percent (%) of indoor woodwork in the contiguous United States in the middle of winter (*top*) and summer (*bottom*).

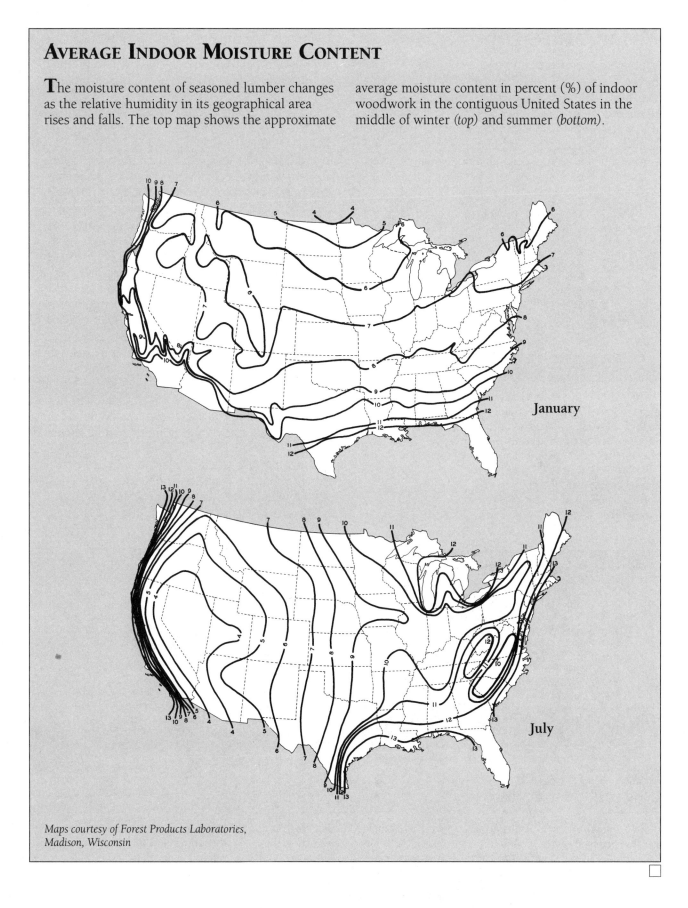

January

July

Maps courtesy of Forest Products Laboratories, Madison, Wisconsin

WOOD STRENGTH

With every woodworking project, you must consider how each part will support a load, if only its own weight. Usually, this is an intuitive judgment. Having used wooden objects all our lives, we know without thinking approximately how thick, wide, or long a chair leg or a tabletop should be. However, there are times when even an experienced craftsman needs to give more thought to this subject to make an intelligent decision.

WOOD GRAIN AND STRENGTH

Grain direction affects wood strength more than any other factor. Wood is a natural polymer — long, parallel strands of cellulose fibers linked by lignin. (Engineers sometimes compare wood to a fiber-reinforced plastic.) The long, unbroken chains of fibers make wood exceptionally strong — they resist stress and spread the load out over their entire length. If you cut these fibers short or arrange the boards so the fibers can't support the load, you sacrifice most of the wood's strength. A rectangular shelving board that's cut so the grain runs through its length will support a lot more books than one of the same size in which the grain runs through the width.

The reason for this is that cellulose is a lot tougher than lignin. Perform this simple experiment: Cut a board ¼ inch thick, 6 inches wide, and 6 inches long. Try to break it across the grain — the cellulose fibers resist the stress, making the task difficult. But when you try to split it along the grain, the lignin separates easily.

Remember this when you lay out wooden parts. Always orient the grain so the fibers absorb the load. Cut the parts so the fibers remain as long as possible. (*SEE FIGURES 1-18 AND 1-19.*)

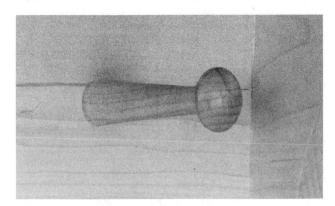

1-18 Although you may never think about it, grain direction is what makes these simple pegs so useful. Because the wood grain runs through the length of each peg, it's able to support well over 1,000 times its own weight. Were the grain to run through the diameter, the peg would easily break off.

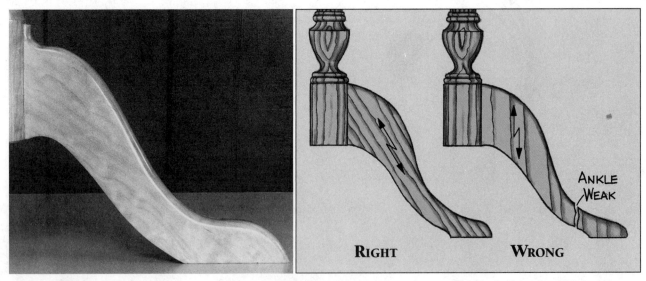

1-19 The wood grain in the legs on this pedestal table is oriented to run parallel to the longest dimen-sion. This makes the legs as strong as possible. If you were to orient the grain vertically, parallel to the pedestal, the legs would be weak at the ankles and the feet would even-tually break off.

RIGHT   WRONG

ANKLE WEAK

SPECIFIC GRAVITY

When strength is paramount, grain direction may not be your only consideration. Some species of wood are stronger than others. Depending on the dimensions of the part and the loads it must support, you may need a relatively strong wood. Windsor chairmakers, for example, traditionally use maple, birch, and hickory for legs, rungs, and spindles. These parts are usually fairly slender, and weaker woods won't hold up.

One of the best indicators of a wood's strength is its *density* — the weight for a given volume. Wood density is commonly measured by its *specific gravity* — the weight of a given volume of wood divided by the weight of the same volume of water. The higher this ratio, the denser — and stronger — the wood. (Because wood is generally less dense than water, the specific gravities for most woods are less than 1. These are written as a decimal. The specific gravity of cherry, for example, is 0.50. Cherry is exactly half as dense as water.) You can look up the specific gravities of common wood species in "Relative Wood Strengths" on page 18.

Note: Specific gravity isn't a failsafe barometer of wood strength. Some woods are stronger than others with slightly higher densities, owing to extractives and other variables. But on the whole, it's a useful reference.

FOR YOUR INFORMATION

Specific gravity can also predict how easily a wood can be worked (its *workability*). The denser the wood, the harder it is to cut, plane, and sand.

OTHER MEASUREMENTS OF STRENGTH

"Strength" can be a nebulous term. To say that cherry is a strong wood doesn't tell you if the surface is strong enough to resist dents and scratches when you use it to make a kitchen counter. Nor does this necessarily mean that a cherry shelf won't sag when it's loaded down with books. For those times when you need more specifics, engineers have devised ways to measure the different types of strengths of wood species. Four of these are of particular interest to craftsmen.

■ *Compressive strength* tells you how much of a load a wood species can withstand parallel to the grain before it fails: How much weight can you put on a table before the legs break?

■ *Bending strength,* or what engineers call *modulus of rupture,* shows how much of a load wood can withstand *perpendicular* to the grain: How much weight can you hang on a wooden peg?

■ It's also helpful to know the *stiffness,* or *modulus of elasticity,* of a species — how much the wood will deflect when a load is applied perpendicular to the grain. This is especially useful when building shelving.

■ Finally, the *hardness* of the wood tells you how resistant the surface is to dents and scratches. This helps you choose durable woods for projects that will likely see a lot of abuse.

The ratings for the various strengths of many common wood species are listed in "Relative Wood Strengths" on page 18.

BUT WAIT, THERE'S MORE!

Grain, movement, and strength aren't the only properties of wood, just the three that most concern craftsmen. There are also decay resistance, chemical resistance, fire resistance, thermal conductivity, electrical conductivity, workability, ease of bending, and so on — more than we have room to discuss here.

If you need information on wood properties that aren't covered here, or you want more details on those properties we have discussed, consult *The Wood Handbook: Wood as an Engineering Material.* This was written for woodworkers and wood manufacturers by the Forest Products Laboratory, a division of the U.S. Department of Agriculture. The prose is as dry as dust, but the book is packed with useful information — it distills over 60 years of wood testing and study at the University of Wisconsin in Madison. Many craftsmen consider it a must-have reference.

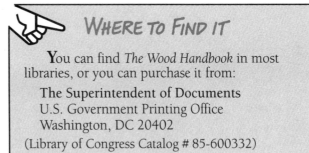

WHERE TO FIND IT

You can find *The Wood Handbook* in most libraries, or you can purchase it from:

The Superintendent of Documents
U.S. Government Printing Office
Washington, DC 20402
(Library of Congress Catalog # 85-600332)

RELATIVE WOOD STRENGTHS

There are several important ways to measure wood strengths. When choosing a wood species, you should first decide what kind of strength you're looking for. Engineers measure the **compressive strength** (1) by loading a block of wood parallel to the grain until it breaks, and the **bending strength** (2) by loading a block perpendicular to the grain. Both are expressed in pounds per square inch (psi).

Stiffness (3) is determined by applying a load to a large beam until it deflects a specific amount. This is usually given in millions of pounds per square inch (Mpsi). To find the **hardness** (4), engineers measure the force needed to drive a metal ball halfway into a wooden surface. This force is recorded in pounds (lbs). In each case, the higher the number, the stronger the wood.

SPECIES	SPECIFIC GRAVITY	COMPRESSIVE STRENGTH (psi)	BENDING STRENGTH (psi)	STIFFNESS (Mpsi)	HARDNESS (lbs)
Domestic Hardwoods					
Alder, Red	.41	5,820	9,800	1.38	590
Ash, White	.60	7,410	15,000	1.74	1,320
Aspen (Cottonwood)	.38	4,250	8,400	1.18	350
Basswood	.37	4,730	8,700	1.46	410
Beech	.64	7,300	14,900	1.72	1,300
Birch, White	.55	5,690	12,300	1.59	910
Birch, Yellow	.62	8,170	16,600	2.01	1,260
Butternut	.38	5,110	8,100	1.18	490
Cherry	.50	7,110	12,300	1.49	950
Chestnut	.43	5,320	8,600	1.23	540
Elm	.50	5,520	11,800	1.34	830
Hickory	.72	9,210	20,200	2.16	N/A*
Maple, Hard	.63	7,830	15,800	1.83	1,450
Maple, Soft	.54	6,540	13,400	1.64	950
Oak, Red	.63	6,760	14,300	1.82	1,290
Oak, White	.68	7,440	15,200	1.78	1,360
Pecan	.66	7,850	13,700	1.73	1,820
Poplar, Yellow	.42	5,540	10,100	1.58	540
Sassafras	.46	4,760	9,000	1.12	N/A*
Sweetgum	.52	6,320	12,500	1.64	850
Sycamore	.49	5,380	10,000	1.42	770
Tupelo	.50	5,520	9,600	1.20	810
Walnut	.55	7,580	14,600	1.68	1,010
Willow	.39	4,100	7,800	1.01	N/A*

* Not available — these woods have not been completely tested.

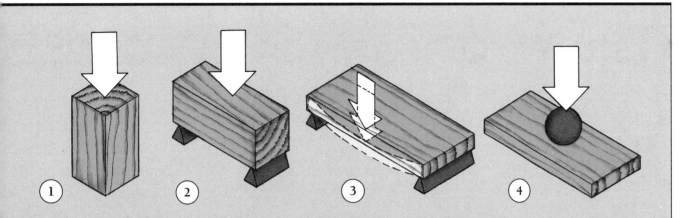

SPECIES	SPECIFIC GRAVITY	COMPRESSIVE STRENGTH (psi)	BENDING STRENGTH (psi)	STIFFNESS (Mpsi)	HARDNESS (lbs)
Domestic Softwoods					
Cedar, Aromatic Red	.47	6,020	8,800	.88	900
Cedar, Western Red	.32	4,560	7,500	1.11	350
Cedar, White	.32	3,960	6,500	.80	320
Cypress	.46	6,360	10,600	1.44	510
Fir, Douglas	.48	7,230	12,400	1.95	710
Hemlock	.45	7,200	11,300	1.63	540
Larch	.52	7,620	13,000	1.87	830
Pine, Ponderosa	.40	5,320	9,400	1.29	460
Pine, Sugar	.36	4,460	8,200	1.19	380
Pine, White	.35	4,800	8,600	1.24	380
Pine, Yellow	.59	8,470	14,500	1.98	870
Redwood	.35	5,220	7,900	1.10	420
Spruce, Sitka	.40	5,610	10,200	1.57	510
Imported Woods					
Bubinga	.71	10,500	22,600	2.48	2,690
Jelutong	.36	3,920	7,300	1.18	390
Lauan	.40	7,360	12,700	1.77	780
Mahogany, African	.42	6,460	10,700	1.40	830
Mahogany, Genuine	.45	6,780	11,500	1.50	800
Primavera	.40	5,600	9,500	1.04	660
Purpleheart	.67	10,320	19,200	2.27	1,860
Rosewood, Brazilian	.80	9,600	19,000	1.88	2,720
Rosewood, Indian	.75	9,220	16,900	1.78	3,170
Teak	.55	8,410	14,600	1.55	1,000

2

HARDWOODS AND SOFTWOODS

Wood is commonly divided up into hardwoods and softwoods. This has little to do with relative hardness of the materials, although as a group, hardwoods rank harder than softwoods. Rather, it denotes a botanical difference between lumber from trees with encased seeds and leaves versus those with cones and needles.

For a woodworker in North America, there are actually three types of wood — domestic hardwoods, domestic softwoods, and imported woods. Most imports are actually hardwoods, but we have come to think of them as a class by themselves. I remember admiring a turned box at a woodworking show — it was made of kingwood, a South American import that I hadn't seen until then. I inspected the grain closely, found the telltale pores that distinguish hardwood from softwood, then asked the turner, "What kind of hardwood is it?"

"It's not a hardwood," he replied, apparently disgusted that I would think it was anything so pedestrian. "It's an *exotic*."

However you want to divide them up, there are over 250 types of lumber commercially available in the United States, and perhaps as many as 1,000 worldwide. Even if you work exclusively with a few species that are available locally, it's fascinating to learn about the incredible variety of woods that are available to you.

WOOD BOTANY

Before reviewing different species, it helps to know some of the botanical traits that set hardwoods and softwoods apart from each other. It's commonly believed that hardwoods come from *deciduous* trees and softwoods come from *conifers*. Basically, this is true, but there's more to it than that.

BIOLOGICAL DIFFERENCES

Hardwood comes from *angiosperms,* which means the plant seeds are encased in a "seed vessel" like a fruit or a nut. There are two types of angiosperms, *monocots* (such as palm and bamboo) and *dicots* (such as oak and rosewood). Almost all hardwoods come from dicots. Most dicots that live in temperate climates are *deciduous,* meaning they lose their leaves during winter dormancy. Dicots in warmer parts of the world don't lose their leaves. So, contrary to the standard definition, not all hardwoods come from deciduous trees.

Softwood comes from *gymnosperms,* plants with naked seeds. (As the seeds develop on the cones, they are not encased in any tissue.) Within this broad classification, there is a subdivision of *conifers,* which are characterized by needle- and scale-like foliage. All softwoods are harvested from coniferous gymnosperms. These botanical categories, while interesting, make little difference to a woodworker. To find those traits that affect your craftsmanship, you have to look closer.

MICROSCOPIC DIFFERENCES

Study a piece of hardwood under a microscope and you'll find four major types of cells (*SEE FIGURE 2-1*). Three of these are longitudinal cells, running parallel to the length of the trunk or branch.

■ Most of the wood tissue is composed of *fibers,* 100 times longer than they are wide. Fibers have very thick cell walls, sometimes appearing almost solid.

■ You may also find a small number of *tracheids,* slightly shorter than fibers, with much thinner cell walls. They are few and far between, and are completely missing in some hardwood species.

■ Interspersed among the fibers and tracheids are *vessel elements*. These appear much larger in diameter and shorter than the other longitudinal cells, and they are always aligned to form long, longitudinal pipelines.

The fourth cell type runs perpendicular to the others.

■ *Ray cells* form radial pipelines running out from the center of the tree.

The grain and texture of a hardwood depend on the size, shape, and number of each cell type. And because there are so many possible combinations, hardwood grain and texture are enormously varied. For example, the rays can grow quite large, producing a pronounced ray fleck in some species. In quarter-sawn oak, for example, rays are the dominant visual element. In other woods, they are barely noticeable.

Vessel elements also have a conspicuous effect. When a vessel element is sliced open, it leaves a tiny hole or hollow in the wood, called a *pore*. Hardwoods with large pores are said to have an *open grain*. Those with extremely small pores (too small to be seen with your naked eye) have a *closed grain*. (*SEE FIGURE 2-2*.) The size of the pores determines the texture of the hardwood. A coarse-grained hardwood has large pores, while a fine-grained hardwood has small ones.

Some hardwoods have a much larger concentration of pores in the springwood — these are described as *ring-porous*. Hardwoods in which the pores are distributed evenly throughout the springwood and the summerwood are *ring-diffuse*. The distribution of pores has an enormous effect on the appearance of a hardwood. Ring-porous hardwoods tend to have a pronounced or *strong* grain.

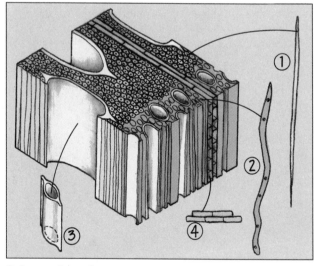

2-1 Hardwoods are composed mainly of four different types of cells. *Fibers* (1), *tracheids* (2), and *vessel elements* (3) are all aligned longitudinally, parallel to the length of the trunk or branch. *Ray cells* (4) align themselves radially, perpendicular to the longitudinal cells.

Softwoods have a simpler structure. (*SEE FIGURE* 2-3.) Between 90 and 95 percent of the wood is composed of tracheids, while the rest are ray cells. There are no fibers or vessel elements, although some softwoods have *resin canals.*

Because there are no fibers in softwoods, they tend not to be as dense or as hard as most hardwoods. And because there are fewer types of cells, there is less variety in the characteristics of softwood grain. For example, the absence of vessel elements eliminates the pores in softwood. The grain is neither ring-porous nor ring-diffuse, neither open nor closed — these terms don't apply to softwoods.

There is, however, a measure of texture. It's determined by the relative size of the tracheids. Softwoods with large cells are said to have a *coarse grain,* while those with small cells have a *fine grain.*

CHEMICAL DIFFERENCES

Although most wood tissue is composed of strands of cellulose stuck together with lignin, there are many other chemicals and minerals embedded in this matrix.

These *extractives,* as the embedded substances are known, differ from species to species. The exact mix is what gives each species of wood its characteristic color. But color is just one of the effects of extractives:

■ Many extractives are minerals that act as fine abrasives, dulling your cutting tools as you work.

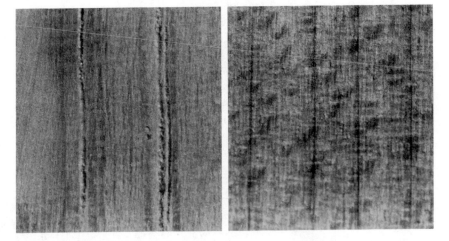

2-2 When you cut through hard-wood, you slice open some of the vessel elements. These appear as tiny *pores* in the wood surface. When these pores are large enough to be seen with the unaided eye, as they are on this white oak (*left*), the wood is said to have an *open grain* and a *coarse* texture. When they are too small to be seen and the wood surface appears smooth, as on this hard maple (*right*), the wood has a *closed grain* and a *fine* texture.

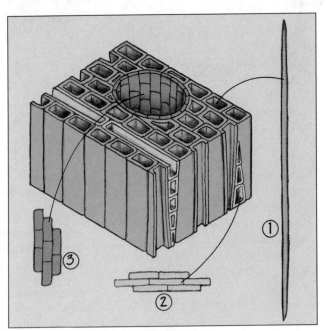

2-3 For the most part, softwoods are composed of just two types of cells — longitudinal *tracheids* (1) and radial *ray cells* (2). A few softwoods may also have *resin canals* (3) lined with thin-walled cells.

■ Some are oily or waxy substances. These build up as *pitch* on the cutting surfaces of power tools and interfere with the cutting action. They can also make a wood difficult to glue or finish.

■ Many are antibiotics, killing molds and bacteria that would cause disease or wood rot. Woods high in these chemicals are resistant to decay.

■ A few of these antibiotic chemicals are toxic to humans as well as microbes and have been known to cause or aggravate allergic reactions, respiratory ailments, and other health problems. For more information on woods that contain potentially dangerous extractives, see "Toxic Woods" on this page.

Toxic Woods

Like many plants, trees produce defensive chemicals to protect themselves from the organisms that prey upon them. Most are concentrated in the leaves, fruit, and bark to ward off browsing animals. But the wood itself may contain antibiotics to help control microbes that cause disease and decay. These chemicals may also have an unpleasant effect on woodworkers and other folks who come into intimate contact with the wood. They have been found to cause or contribute to:

■ Nausea and headaches
■ Kidney and liver malfunction
■ Skin rashes and eye irritation
■ Asthma, emphysema, and other respiratory problems
■ Nasal cancer

Before this problem gets blown out of proportion, let me assure you that not everyone is affected by the potentially toxic chemicals in wood. Only 2 to 5 people out of 100 ever develop an unhealthy sensitivity to them, although woodworkers do have an increased risk. And not many woods contain enough of these chemicals to be dangerous. There are just a few bad boys that you should be especially concerned about — these are listed in "Troublesome Woods" on page 24.

There are two common ways that wood can affect your health — either as an *irritant* or a *sensitizer*. Irritants bother most woodworkers, at least to a small degree. These effects may be mechanical rather than chemical — fine sawdust will tickle your nasal passages and cause you to sneeze. More often, though, it's the chemicals in the sawdust that irritate various parts of your body. The tannic acid in oak, for example, is a powerful irritant.

Sensitizers affect only those people who are allergic to them. If you are one of these few, contact with a sensitizing chemical causes an allergic reaction, which can range from a runny nose and watery eyes to hives and asthma. Furthermore, repeated exposure often causes greater sensitivity, and the reaction becomes more severe.

A very few woods contain chemicals which cause *systemic* reactions, affecting the stomach, nerves, kidneys, and even the heart. Oleander and yew, for example, contain chemicals similar to digitalis, a heart drug.

What can you do to limit your exposure to these chemicals, other than avoiding woods that make you uncomfortable? Quite a bit.

■ Whenever you're kicking up sawdust, wear a dust mask. The primary way in which toxic wood chemicals get into your body is through inhalation.

■ Use a dust collector when running power tools.

■ Make sure your shop is well ventilated and clean it frequently to keep down the level of sawdust.

■ Keep your shop cool. Heat causes you to perspire and the perspiration mixes with sawdust, releasing more of the toxic chemicals.

Also, try not to expose other people to these chemicals. Never use potentially toxic woods to make cutting boards, bowls, platters, or any utensil that might come into contact with food. Also avoid these woods for toys, jewelry, or any other object that someone might put in their mouth or rub against their skin.

One more important caution: See a doctor if you have persistent health problems when you work with wood. A constant runny nose, recurrent nosebleeds, or persistent sinus infections are causes for special concern.

(continued) ▷

Toxic Woods — continued

Troublesome Woods

Species	Irritant	Sensitizer	Species	Irritant	Sensitizer
Cedar, Western red	No	Yes	Oak, red and white	Yes	No
Cocobolo	Yes	No	Oleander	Yes	No
Ebony	Yes	Maybe	Paduak	Yes	No
Fir, Douglas	Yes	Maybe	Peroba Rosa	Yes	Maybe
Goncalo alves	No	Yes	Rosewood, Brazilian	No	Yes
Ipe	No	Yes	Rosewood, Indian	No	Yes
Iroko	Yes	Maybe	Sassafras	Yes	Maybe
Kingwood	No	Yes	Satinwood	Yes	No
Lacewood			Spruce	No	Yes
(Silky oak)	Yes	Maybe	Teak	No	Yes
Mansonia			Tulipwood	No	Yes
(African walnut)	Yes	Yes	Walnut	Yes	Maybe
Myrtle, Oregon	Yes	Maybe	Yew	Yes	No

Thanks to Jon Arno of Durst Lumber for his help in preparing this chart.

Wood Characteristics and Uses

IMPORTANT PROPERTIES

When you work with a wood species, it helps to know its specific characteristics. So far in this book, we've discussed two important *mechanical* properties of wood (movement and strength), as well as the most prominent *physical* properties (color, texture, and grain pattern). Each species also has *working* properties — the ease with which you can cut it with hand and power tools, glue it together, and finish it.

It's useful to know these characteristics when you are choosing a wood for a project. Even if you have worked with a species all your life, you can learn something new about it by comparing its properties with those of other woods. To help you do this, I've assembled the following reference list of commercially available woods. Each entry has a brief description of the wood's mechanical, physical, and working properties, as well as its common uses and other important traits.

The mechanical properties include:

■ *Hardness,* or the ability of the wood surface to resist damage. Woods are rated as very hard, hard, soft, and very soft.

■ *Strength,* a summary of compressive strength, bending strength, and stiffness (shown in "Relative Wood Strengths" on page 18). The ratings are very strong, strong, weak, and very weak.

■ *Movement,* a summary of tangential and radial movement (shown in "Tangential and Radial Movement" on page 14). The ratings are very stable, stable, unstable, and very unstable.

The physical properties are:

■ *Color,* usually just the predominate hue and shade, unless the wood is streaked or there is a striking difference between the heartwood and sapwood.

■ *Texture,* which may be coarse, medium-coarse, medium, medium-fine, or fine.

■ *Grain,* which may be straight, irregular, wavy, or interlocked. In interlocking grain, the grain direction spirals up the trunk, reversing direction with each growth ring. (*See Figure 2-4.*)

And the working properties consist of:

■ The relative ease of working the wood species with both **hand tools** and **power tools**. These are rated as very easy, easy, difficult, and very difficult.

■ The relative ease of *gluing* and *finishing* the wood. These are rated as excellent, good, adequate, and poor.

I've also included the *specific gravity* for each wood, since this is a good indicator of many mechanical, physical, and working properties, such as hardness, strength, weight, density, and general workability.

Knowing the specific gravities of different woods can also help compare a species you're not familiar with to one whose characteristics you know well. (See "Relative Wood Strengths" on page 18 for more information on this important trait.)

Unfortunately, there isn't room to discuss all the available species. For information on woods that aren't listed here, consult *The Wood Handbook* from the Forest Products Laboratory. (Refer to page 17.)

DOMESTIC HARDWOODS

ALDER, RED

Other Common Name: Western alder
Sources: Western North America
Specific Gravity: 0.41
Mechanical Properties: Very soft, very weak, and unstable.
Physical Properties: Pale red-brown, sometimes with a yellow tint. Has a fine texture and straight grain.
Working Properties: Difficult to work with hand tools and power tools because the grain tears easily. Good for both gluing and finishing.
Common Uses: Utility wood for furniture.
Comments: Blends with walnut, mahogany, and cherry when stained. Used extensively in framing upholstered furniture because it holds tacks well.

ASH

Other Common Names: White ash, Brown ash
Sources: Most of North America, except extremely cold regions
Specific Gravity: 0.60
Mechanical Properties: Hard, strong, and unstable. Also shock resistant.
Physical Properties: Usually light tan, although some trees yield medium brown wood. Has a coarse texture and straight grain.
Working Properties: Very easy to work with hand tools, and easy with power tools. Excellent for gluing and finishing.
Common Uses: Ball bats, hockey sticks, tool handles, cabinets, bentwood furniture, food containers.
Comments: Popular for food containers because the wood imparts no taste to the food.

ASPEN

Other Common Names: Quivering or Quaking aspen, Cottonwood
Sources: Most of North America
Specific Gravity: 0.38

Mechanical Properties: Very soft, very weak, and unstable.
Physical Properties: Light tan, sometimes with a gray cast. Has a fine texture and straight grain.
Working Properties: Very easy to work with hand tools, easy with power tools. Good for gluing, but poor for finishing.
Common Uses: Used mostly to make paper. Lumber is used as a utility wood and is sometimes substituted for basswood.
Comments: Although aspen isn't the same species as eastern cottonwood, the two are almost indistinguishable in lumber form and are used interchangeably.

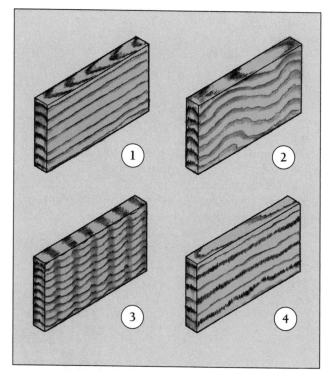

2-4 Wood grain is characterized by the pattern shown in the quarter grain. Although there are many possible patterns, they all fall into four major categories. *Straight grain* (1), which is the most common, shows reasonably straight, parallel lines. *Irregular grain* (2) has no regular pattern. *Wavy grain* (3) often produces a curly figure — the lines are parallel but they meander back and forth. *Interlocked grain* (4) shows up as ribbon figure. This occurs when the grain spirals around the trunk, reversing direction with each growth ring.

BASSWOOD

Other Common Names: American lime, Linden
Sources: Eastern North America
Specific Gravity: 0.37
Mechanical Properties: Very soft, very weak, and very unstable.
Physical Properties: Creamy white with an extremely fine texture and straight grain.
Working Properties: Very easy to work with hand tools and power tools. Excellent for gluing and finishing.
Common Uses: Carving, toys, moldings, eating and cooking utensils, boxes, beehives.
Comments: Despite its instability, this wood is preferred by many carvers because it's easy to work and has a very consistent grain that holds detail well.

BEECH

Other Common Names: None
Sources: Eastern North America
Specific Gravity: 0.64
Mechanical Properties: Very hard, very strong, and very unstable. It also resists abrasion better than most woods.
Physical Properties: Light brown to reddish brown, with a medium texture and straight grain.
Working Properties: Easy to work with hand tools and power tools, although the wood burns easily when using high-speed cutters. Excellent for gluing and finishing.

Common Uses: Cabinets, bentwood furniture, tool handles, boxes, flooring. Sometimes substituted for hard maple.
Comments: Good for bending.

BIRCH, PAPER

Other Common Names: White birch, Canoe birch
Sources: Eastern North America
Specific Gravity: 0.55
Mechanical Properties: Hard, strong, and very unstable.
Physical Properties: Creamy white sapwood, pale brown heartwood, fine texture, and straight grain.
Working Properties: Easy to work with hand tools and power tools. Excellent for gluing and finishing.
Common Uses: Dowels, spools, toothpicks, clothespins, light-use tool handles (such as brush handles).
Comments: The sapwood is highly prized for commercial turnings.

BIRCH, YELLOW (SEE FIGURE 2-5.)

Other Common Name: Hard birch
Sources: Eastern North America
Specific Gravity: 0.62
Mechanical Properties: Very hard, very strong, and very unstable.
Physical Properties: Yellow-tan sapwood and red-brown heartwood. Boards often show a good deal of variation in color. Has a medium texture with mostly straight grain. Often shows curly figure.

2-5 Yellow birch is a good choice for utility built-ins and storage projects because it's durable and relatively inexpensive. These shop cabinets are made from birch and birch plywood.

Working Properties: Straight-grained wood is easy to work with hand tools and power tools. Excellent for gluing and finishing.

Common Uses: Furniture, bentwood furniture, cabinets, flooring, windows, doors, interior trim.

Comments: Good for bending and often used as a face veneer on cabinet-grade plywood. An extremely versatile wood.

BUTTERNUT

Other Common Name: White walnut
Sources: Northeastern North America
Specific Gravity: 0.38
Mechanical Properties: Very soft, very weak, and stable.
Physical Properties: Light brown color, medium-coarse texture, and can have both straight and irregular grain.
Working Properties: Very easy to work with both hand tools and power tools. Excellent for gluing and finishing. Resembles light-colored walnut.
Common Uses: Carving, furniture, wall paneling.
Comments: Once a common source of dye — our pioneer ancestors often wore "butternut jeans."

CHERRY (*See Figure 2-6.*)

Other Common Names: Black cherry, Fruitwood
Sources: Eastern North America, mostly the Appalachian states
Specific Gravity: 0.50
Mechanical Properties: Hard, strong, and very stable.
Physical Properties: Pinkish sapwood and red heartwood that darkens with age — sapwood is sometimes considered a defect because the color difference is so striking. Has a fine texture and straight grain, although wavy grain is not uncommon. May also have small, dark sap pockets.
Working Properties: Straight-grained wood is very easy to work with hand tools. Easy to work with power tools, although the wood is sometimes brittle and chips easily. It also burns easily when using high-speed cutters. Excellent for gluing and finishing.
Common Uses: Furniture, cabinets.
Comments: Considered a premium furniture wood.

CHESTNUT

Other Common Name: Wormy chestnut
Sources: Southeastern North America
Specific Gravity: 0.43
Mechanical Properties: Soft, weak, and very stable.
Physical Properties: Light brown with a coarse texture and straight grain. Almost always full of bore holes.

Working Properties: Very easy to work with hand tools and power tools. Excellent for gluing and finishing.

Common Uses: Furniture, antique reproduction.

Comments: Was once an important furniture wood until a parasitic fungus destroyed most of the living trees in the early part of the twentieth century. New lumber is sometimes salvaged from standing dead trees or old barn timbers. These have usually been attacked by insects over the years; hence the worm holes.

ELM

Other Common Names: White elm, Soft elm
Sources: Eastern North America
Specific Gravity: 0.50
Mechanical Properties: Hard, weak, and unstable.
Physical Properties: Tan, coarse texture, and both straight and irregular grain.
Working Properties: Difficult to work with both hand tools and power tools — you have to keep the cutting edges very sharp. Adequate for gluing and finishing.

2-6 Cherry is a fine furniture wood, used for both classic and contemporary styles. It ordinarily has a straight grain, but figured cherry is not uncommon. This fretwork mirror was made from curly cherry.

Common Uses: Cabinets, furniture, chair seats, bentwood furniture, boats, barrels, baskets.
Comments: Fairly good for bending.

HICKORY

Other Common Name: Shagbark hickory
Sources: Eastern North America
Specific Gravity: 0.72
Mechanical Properties: Very hard, very strong, and very unstable.
Physical Properties: Light brown, medium-coarse texture, and mostly straight grain.
Working Properties: Very difficult to work with hand tools, and difficult to work with power tools. Excellent for gluing and good for finishing.
Common Uses: Tool handles, pegs, athletic equipment, and ladder rungs.
Comments: Also used to smoke meats.

HOLLY

Other Common Names: None
Sources: Southeastern North America
Specific Gravity: 0.50
Mechanical Properties: Hard, strong, and unstable.
Physical Properties: Chalky white with a fine texture and straight grain.
Working Properties: Very easy to work with hand tools and power tools. Excellent for gluing and finishing.

Common Uses: Inlays, marquetry, musical instruments.
Comments: Holly is an evergreen dicot — one of the few domestic hardwood trees that doesn't lose its leaves.

MAPLE, HARD *(See Figure 2-7.)*

Other Common Names: Rock maple, Sugar maple
Sources: Eastern North America
Specific Gravity: 0.63
Mechanical Properties: Very hard, very strong, and unstable.
Physical Properties: Light tan sapwood, light brown heartwood, fine texture, and mostly straight grain. However, figured grain is common. Sawyers often sort maple for curly, bird's-eye, and quilted figure.
Working Properties: Difficult to work with hand tools because the wood is so hard; easy to work with power tools, although high-speed cutters will burn it. Adequate for gluing, excellent for finishing.
Common Uses: Furniture, chair legs and rungs, turnings, flooring, musical instruments, cutting boards, toys, eating and cooking utensils.
Comments: Figured hard maple is considered a premium furniture wood.

MAPLE, SOFT *(See Figure 2-8.)*

Other Common Name: Red maple
Sources: Eastern North America

2-7 Hard maple is an extremely durable wood and is often used for butcherblocks, countertops, and other surfaces that must take a beating. This cabinetmaker's workbench is made from hard maple.

Specific Gravity: 0.54

Mechanical Properties: Hard, strong, and stable.

Physical Properties: Sapwood is tan, heartwood can be dark tan to red-brown. Medium-fine texture and mostly straight grain. Grain is sometimes figured, although figure isn't as common in soft maple as it is in hard maple.

Working Properties: Difficult to work with hand tools, easy to work with power tools, although high-speed cutters burn it easily. Good for gluing and excellent for finishing.

Common Uses: Furniture, turnings, boxes, toys, eating and cooking utensils.

Comments: The name is somewhat misleading — soft maple is harder than many hardwoods, and only slightly softer than hard maple.

OAK, RED

Other Common Names: None

Sources: North America

Specific Gravity: 0.63

Mechanical Properties: Very hard, strong, and very unstable.

Physical Properties: Pink-tan with a coarse texture and straight grain, although curly grain is not unheard of. Has a striking quarter grain showing large "silvery" rays.

Working Properties: Easy to work with hand tools and power tools as long as you keep them sharp. Good for gluing and finishing.

Common Uses: Furniture, cabinets, flooring, interior trim, boxes, railways ties, structural timbers.

Comments: Potentially toxic — high tannin content makes red oak dust a powerful irritant.

OAK, WHITE (*See Figure 2-9.*)

Other Common Names: None

Sources: North America

Specific Gravity: 0.68

Mechanical Properties: Very hard, strong, and very unstable.

Physical Properties: Tan, with coarse texture and straight grain. Curly grain is rare, but not unheard of, and quarter grain shows large "silvery" rays.

Working Properties: Easy to work with hand tools and power tools, provided you keep them sharp. Wood can be brittle and has a tendency to chip, and high-speed cutters burn it easily. Good for gluing and finishing.

Common Uses: Furniture, cabinets, flooring, interior trim, structural timbers, boxes, barrels.

Comments: Together, white and red oak are the most widely used hardwoods in North America.

PECAN

Other Common Name: Sweet pecan

Sources: Southeastern North America

Specific Gravity: 0.66

Mechanical Properties: Very hard, strong, and unstable. Also abrasion resistant.

Physical Properties: Creamy white sapwood and red-tan heartwood, although the colors vary somewhat. Has a medium texture and straight grain.

Working Properties: Difficult to work with hand tools because it's so hard and dense. Moderately difficult with power tools — dulls cutting edges quickly. Adequate for gluing, good for finishing.

Common Uses: Furniture, tool handles, sports equipment, flooring.

Comments: Sometimes substituted for hickory.

POPLAR, YELLOW (*See Figure 2-10.*)

Other Common Name: Tulip tree

Sources: Eastern North America

Specific Gravity: 0.42

2-8 Both hard and soft maple are often highly figured, especially if the trees grow in a cold climate. This tip-and-turn table is made from quilted soft maple.

Mechanical Properties: Soft, strong, and stable.

Physical Properties: Creamy white sapwood, yellow-green heartwood, sometimes streaked with black and purple. Has a medium-fine texture and straight grain.

Working Properties: Very easy to work with hand tools and power tools. Excellent for gluing, good for finishing. Holds paint well.

Common Uses: Furniture, cabinets, ladders, pattern-making, turning, musical instruments, boxes, eating and cooking utensils, toys, interior and exterior trim, siding, structural timbers. An extremely versatile wood, there's not much it isn't used for.

Comments: Should not be confused with tulipwood, an imported member of the rosewood family.

SWEET GUM

Other Common Names: Red gum, Hazel
Sources: Southeastern North America
Specific Gravity: 0.52
Mechanical Properties: Hard, strong, and unstable.
Physical Properties: Red-brown, medium texture, and irregular grain.
Working Properties: Difficult to work with hand tools because of the irregular grain, but easy to work with power tools. Excellent for gluing, good for finishing.
Common Uses: Furniture, cabinets.

SYCAMORE

Other Common Name: Buttonwood
Sources: Eastern North America
Specific Gravity: 0.49
Mechanical Properties: Hard, strong, and unstable. Also very tough — wears well.
Physical Properties: Pink-brown, medium texture, straight grain. Quarter grain shows a striking "lacy" ray pattern.
Working Properties: Difficult to work with hand tools and power tools because the grain tears easily. Excellent for gluing, good for finishing.
Common Uses: Furniture, cabinets, food containers.
Comments: Sometimes substituted for maple when weight is a consideration.

TUPELO

Other Common Name: Black gum
Sources: Eastern North America
Specific Gravity: 0.46
Mechanical Properties: Hard, weak, and unstable.
Physical Properties: Pale brown with a fine texture and irregular grain.
Working Properties: Easy to work with hand tools and power tools. Excellent for gluing, good for finishing.

2-9 Oak was a popular fine furniture wood when this country was first settled, but it was soon eclipsed by walnut, cherry, figured maple, and imported mahogany. However, it became an important furniture wood again during the nineteenth century, as furnituremakers adopted factory techniques. Oak was abundant, inexpensive, easily seasoned, and easy to machine — a manufacturer's dream. So much oak furniture was made during the late nineteenth century that the prevalent style of the time is sometimes called "Victorian Oak" or simply "Oak." This rolltop desk, made from white oak, is a typical example.

Common Uses: Principally used to make paper, but lumber also serves as a utility wood for furniture, millwork, and boxes.

WALNUT *(See Figure 2-11.)*

Other Common Name: Black walnut
Sources: Eastern North America
Specific Gravity: 0.55
Mechanical Properties: Hard, strong, and stable.
Physical Properties: Tan sapwood, dark brown heartwood, has a medium texture and mostly straight grain. Crotch figure can be stunning. Sapwood is sometimes considered a defect because it's so much lighter than the heartwood. Sawyers often "steam dry" the lumber — this partially dissolves the extractives in the heartwood and dyes the sapwood to match.
Working Properties: Very easy to work with hand tools and power tools. Good for gluing, excellent for finishing.

Common Uses: Furniture, cabinets, gun stocks.
Comments: The taproot is extremely hard and highly figured — sometimes this is used for gun stocks. Considered a premium furniture wood. Potentially toxic.

WILLOW

Other Common Name: Black willow
Sources: Eastern North America
Specific Gravity: 0.39
Mechanical Properties: Very soft, very weak, and stable.
Physical Properties: Dark brown (although color can vary), coarse texture, and straight grain.
Working Properties: Very easy to work with hand tools and power tools. Excellent for gluing, good for finishing.
Common Uses: Furniture, boxes, toys, beehives.
Comments: Sometimes stained to simulate walnut.

2-10 Although poplar is normally thought of as a utility wood, it can be used as a primary wood to build some very fine furniture. It's especially good for painted and lacquered furniture, such as this painted stepback cupboard. *Photo courtesy of The Workshops of David T. Smith.*

DOMESTIC SOFTWOODS

CEDAR, AROMATIC RED (SEE FIGURE 2-12.)

Other Common Name: Juniper
Sources: Southeastern North America
Specific Gravity: 0.47
Mechanical Properties: Hard, weak, and stable.
Physical Properties: White sapwood, pink or red heartwood, fine texture, and irregular grain. Also has a distinct smell.
Working Properties: Easy to work with hand tools unless wood is knotty. Very easy to work with power tools. Good for gluing and finishing.
Common Uses: Boxes, chests, liners for closets and storage units.
Comments: Not really a cedar — belongs to the same family as cypress.

CEDAR, WESTERN RED

Other Common Name: Arborvitae
Sources: Western North America
Specific Gravity: 0.32
Mechanical Properties: Very soft, very weak, and very stable.
Physical Properties: Red-brown, with a medium texture and straight grain.
Working Properties: Very easy to work with hand tools and power tools. Excellent for gluing, good for finishing.

Common Uses: Shingles, doors, windows, interior and exterior trim, small boats, decking, fencing, outdoor furniture.
Comments: Decay resistant, potentially toxic.

CEDAR, WHITE (SEE FIGURE 2-13.)

Other Common Names: Atlantic white cedar, Post cedar
Sources: Southeastern North America
Specific Gravity: 0.31
Mechanical Properties: Very soft, very weak, and very stable.
Physical Properties: Pale pink-brown, with a fine texture and straight grain.
Working Properties: Very easy to work with hand tools and power tools. Excellent for gluing, good for finishing.
Common Uses: Shingles, boats, millwork, eating and cooking utensils, outdoor furniture.
Comments: Resists decay.

CYPRESS

Other Common Name: Bald cypress
Sources: Southeastern North America
Specific Gravity: 0.46
Mechanical Properties: Hard, strong, and stable.

2-11 **Walnut is one of our most** valuable furniture woods because it works so easily and finishes elegantly. Unfortunately, current wood manufacturing practices — steam drying, in particular — mute its natural colors. Air-dried walnut, if you can find it, has a much richer color and grain pattern. This library table was crafted from air-dried walnut.

2-12 Aromatic cedar, because of its unique smell, has spawned a lot of folklore. It's generally believed that the odor repels insects, although there is no evidence that it does so. A butter plate made from cedar is thought to keep the butter fresh, but there is no proof of this, either. Some woodworkers believe that Arkansas sharpening stones are best stored in cedar boxes, but the cedar does nothing for the stone. Arkansas stones are often shipped in cedar boxes simply because there's a lot of cedar in Arkansas.

Physical Properties: Orange-brown, with medium-coarse texture and straight grain.

Working Properties: Very easy to work with hand tools and power tools. Excellent for gluing, good for finishing. Takes paint well.

Common Uses: Cabinets, paneling, millwork, furniture.

Comments: Not to be confused with genuine cypress, a hardwood. Genuine cypress was depleted in the mid-twentieth century; bald cypress makes an acceptable substitute. Resistant to decay.

FIR, DOUGLAS

Other Common Name: Oregon pine
Sources: Western North America
Specific Gravity: 0.48
Mechanical Properties: Hard, strong, and stable.
Physical Properties: Pale red-brown with a coarse texture and straight grain.
Working Properties: Easy to work with hand tools, very easy with machine tools. Good for gluing, but difficult to finish because the surface is hard to prepare — the summerwood stands proud after you sand it.
Common Uses: Construction lumber, millwork, interior trim, flooring.

HEMLOCK

Other Common Name: Western hemlock
Sources: Western North America
Specific Gravity: 0.45
Mechanical Properties: Hard, strong, and unstable.

2-13 White cedar is an excellent wood for outdoor furniture, such as this Adirondack chair. Even though it's soft and weak, it's highly resistant to decay. Several craftsmen on the Atlantic coast have told me it's one of the few woods they have found that will stand up to salt water.

Physical Properties: Tan, with a coarse texture and both straight and irregular grain.

Working Properties: Very easy to work with hand tools and power tools. Excellent for gluing, good for finishing.

Common Uses: Construction lumber. Sometimes used as a substitute for pine and poplar.

Comments: No relation to poisonous herb hemlock.

LARCH

Other Common Name: Western larch
Sources: Western North America
Specific Gravity: 0.52
Mechanical Properties: Hard, very strong, and unstable.

Physical Properties: Orange-red with a coarse texture and both straight and irregular grain.

Working Properties: Easy to work with hand tools, very easy with power tools. Good for gluing, difficult to finish because surface is hard to prepare — the summerwood stands proud after sanding.

Common Uses: Doors, windows, flooring, boats, fencing.

PINE, PONDEROSA

Other Common Names: Bull pine, Knotty pine
Sources: Western North America
Specific Gravity: 0.40
Mechanical Properties: Soft, strong, and stable.

Physical Properties: Sapwood is pale yellow, heart-wood is pale red-brown. Has a medium-fine texture and mostly straight grain. Lumber can be knotty.

Working Properties: Knot-free lumber is easy to work with hand tools, very easy with power tools. Excellent for gluing, good for finishing.

Common Uses: Construction lumber, millwork, cabinets, interior trim, paneling.

PINE, SUGAR

Other Common Names: None
Sources: Western North America
Specific Gravity: 0.36
Mechanical Properties: Very soft, weak, and very stable.

Physical Properties: Tan, with a fine texture and straight grain.

Working Properties: Easy to work with hand tools, very easy with power tools. Excellent for gluing, good for finishing.

Common Uses: Carving, millwork, pattern-making, boxes, construction lumber.

PINE, WHITE (*See Figure 2-14.*)

Other Common Names: Northern white pine, Cork pine
Sources: Eastern North America
Specific Gravity: 0.35
Mechanical Properties: Very soft, weak, and very stable.

Physical Properties: Pale tan, with a fine texture and straight grain.

Working Properties: Very easy to work with hand tools and power tools. Excellent for gluing and finishing.

Common Uses: Furniture, millwork, pattern-making, carving, interior trim.

Comments: This was once the most commercially important timber in the United States, but overuse has depleted the supply.

PINE, YELLOW

Other Common Name: Southern yellow pine
Sources: Southeastern North America
Specific Gravity: 0.59
Mechanical Properties: Very hard, strong, and stable.

Physical Properties: Yellow-tan, with a coarse texture and straight grain.

Working Properties: Easy to work with hand tools, although this can vary. Easy to work with power tools, but pitch loads on the cutters. Good for gluing and finishing, yet this can vary, too.

Common Uses: Construction lumber, paper.

Comments: "Yellow pine" is a blanket term that covers many different southeastern pines. Consequently, the working qualities of these species vary widely, depending on the wood and where it was grown.

REDWOOD

Other Common Name: Sequoia
Sources: Western North America
Specific Gravity: 0.35
Mechanical Properties: Very soft, strong, and very stable.

Physical Properties: Red-brown, with medium-fine texture and straight grain.

Working Properties: Very easy to work with both hand tools and power tools. Excellent for gluing, good for finishing.

Common Uses: Shingles, siding, decking, structural timbers.

Comments: Resists decay. Redwoods are the largest and oldest of trees, growing up to 350 feet high and 4,000 years old. So far as is known, none have ever died of old age.

SPRUCE, SITKA

Other Common Name: Silver spruce
Sources: Western North America
Specific Gravity: 0.40
Mechanical Properties: Soft, strong, and stable.
Physical Properties: Pink-tan, with medium-coarse texture and straight grain.
Working Properties: Easy to work with hand tools, difficult with power tools because the grain tears easily. Excellent for gluing, good for finishing.
Common Uses: Construction lumber, boats, aircraft, musical instruments.
Comments: Potentially toxic.

IMPORTED WOODS (EXOTICS)

BOCOTE (*SEE FIGURE 2-15.*)

Other Common Name: Cordia
Sources: Central and South America
Specific Gravity: Not available
Mechanical Properties: Very hard, strong, and stable.
Physical Properties: Streaked with colors that vary from yellow-tan to dark red-brown. Has a medium texture and both straight and interlocking grain.
Working Properties: Straight-grained wood is easy to work with hand tools, easy with power tools. Adequate for gluing, excellent for finishing.

> ## A BIT OF ADVICE
>
> **M**any useful wood species, especially those from fragile environments such as rain forests, are endangered due to overuse and poor management. These are specified as "Endangered" in the Imported Woods list. If you work with these woods, purchase them from a responsible supplier who respects the sensitive environments from which they come. For a list of these suppliers, ask for the "Good Wood" list from:
>
> Woodworker's Alliance for Rainforest
>   Protection
> Box 133
> Coos Bay, OR 97420

Common Uses: Furniture, inlay, tools handles, turnings. Can be substituted for rosewood.

BUBINGA

Other Common Name: African rosewood
Sources: Western Africa
Specific Gravity: 0.71
Mechanical Properties: Very hard, very strong, and stable.
Physical Properties: Deep maroon, with a fine texture and both straight and irregular grain.

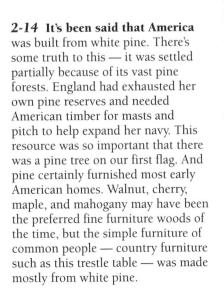

2-14 It's been said that America was built from white pine. There's some truth to this — it was settled partially because of its vast pine forests. England had exhausted her own pine reserves and needed American timber for masts and pitch to help expand her navy. This resource was so important that there was a pine tree on our first flag. And pine certainly furnished most early American homes. Walnut, cherry, maple, and mahogany may have been the preferred fine furniture woods of the time, but the simple furniture of common people — country furniture such as this trestle table — was made mostly from white pine.

Working Properties: Straight-grained wood is easy to work with hand tools and power tools, as long as they are kept sharp. Poor for gluing, excellent for finishing.

Common Uses: Furniture, turnings, eating and cooking utensils.

Comments: Endangered. Gum pockets make it difficult to glue.

COCOBOLO

Other Common Name: Granadillo
Sources: Central America
Specific Gravity: Not available
Mechanical Properties: Very hard, very strong, and stable.

Physical Properties: Streaked with orange-red and brown. Has a medium texture and interlocking grain.

Working Properties: Difficult to work with both hand tools and power tools — the extremely hard wood dulls cutting edges quickly. Oils in the wood make it poor for gluing. Excellent for finishing, although the oils may react with some oil-based finishes.

2-15 The handles and wooden parts of fine tools were once made from rosewood. But as supplies of rosewood have become depleted, manufacturers have begun to offer substitutes. This marking gauge is made from one of the most popular rosewood substitutes, bocote.

Common Uses: Turnings, handles, veneer.
Comments: Endangered. Can be substituted for rosewood. Potentially toxic.

EBONY

Other Common Name: Ebans
Sources: Africa, India, Malaysia, Indonesia
Specific Gravity: 0.95
Mechanical Properties: Very hard, very strong, and very stable.

Physical Properties: Color runs from dark brown to black, although some ebony has black, tan, and gray streaks. Has a fine texture and both straight and irregular grain.

Working Properties: Working this wood with hand tools is beyond difficult, and it's no picnic working it with power tools, either. The wood dulls cutters quickly and chips easily. Poor for gluing, excellent for finishing.

Common Uses: Musical instruments, turnings, handles, inlay.

Comments: Endangered. The supplies of this wood are severely depleted; use alternatives when you can.

GONCALO ALVES

Other Common Name: Tigerwood
Sources: Central America, South America
Specific Gravity: 0.84
Mechanical Properties: Very hard, very strong, and stable.

Physical Properties: Streaked dark brown and orange-red, with a coarse texture and interlocking grain.

Working Properties: Difficult to work with both hand tools and power tools because of the hardness and interlocking grain. Good for gluing, excellent for finishing.

Common Uses: Furniture, turnings, veneer, handles.
Comments: Endangered. A relative of poison ivy and potentially toxic.

JELUTONG *(See Figure 2-16.)*

Other Common Names: None
Sources: Indonesia, Malaysia
Specific Gravity: 0.36
Mechanical Properties: Very soft, very weak, and stable.

Physical Properties: Pale tan, with an extremely fine texture and straight grain.

Working Properties: Very easy to work with both hand tools and power tools. Excellent for gluing and finishing.

Common Uses: Carving, pattern-making.

Comments: Becoming a favorite among carvers. It has many of the same qualities as basswood and is more stable.

LAUAN

Other Common Name: Philippine mahogany
Sources: Indonesia, Malaysia
Specific Gravity: 0.40
Mechanical Properties: Soft, strong, and stable.
Physical Properties: Pale red-brown, with a medium texture and both straight and interlocking grain. Some lauans are darker than others. They are sold as "dark red" or "light red."
Working Properties: Straight-grained wood is very easy to work with hand tools and power tools. Excellent for gluing and finishing.
Common Uses: Furniture, cabinets, boats, boxes, millwork, paneling.
Comments: Resists decay. A premium furniture wood.

MAHOGANY, AFRICAN

Other Common Name: Khaya
Sources: Western Africa
Specific Gravity: 0.42
Mechanical Properties: Soft, strong, and very stable.
Physical Properties: Red-brown, with a medium texture and interlocking grain. Often displays a ribbon figure.
Working Properties: Very easy to work with both hand tools and power tools. Excellent for gluing and finishing.

Common Uses: Furniture, veneer. Can be substituted for genuine mahogany.

MAHOGANY, GENUINE (*See Figure* 2-17.)

Other Common Names: Honduras mahogany, Central American mahogany
Sources: Central America, Northern South America
Specific Gravity: 0.45
Mechanical Properties: Hard, strong, and very stable.
Physical Properties: Red-brown, with a medium texture and both straight and interlocking grain. Sometimes displays ribbon figure; crotch figure is spectacular.
Working Properties: Very easy to work with both hand tools and power tools. Excellent for gluing and finishing.
Common Uses: Furniture, antique reproductions, carving, veneer, outdoor furniture. A premium furniture wood, preferred for classic styles (Queen Anne, Chippendale, and Federal).
Comments: Endangered. Resists decay.

PADUAK

Other Common Name: Vermillion
Sources: Western Africa
Specific Gravity: Not available
Mechanical Properties: Very hard, strong, and unstable.
Physical Properties: Vivid red-orange to start, but darkens to a dark purple-brown with exposure. Coarse texture and both straight and irregular grain.

2-16 Jelutong is one of the best carving woods not because it's soft, but because it's consistent. Unlike other woods, there's almost no difference between springwood and summerwood, so you can control your carving tool very precisely as you push it through the growth rings at an even pace. These pull toys were carved from jelutong.

Working Properties: Straight-grained wood is easy to work with hand tools, very easy with power tools. Good for gluing, excellent for finishing.

Common Uses: Furniture, turnings, handles.

Comments: Endangered.

PRIMAVERA

Other Common Name: White mahogany

Sources: Central America

Specific Gravity: 0.40

Mechanical Properties: Soft, weak, and very stable.

Physical Properties: Creamy white, with a medium texture and both straight and interlocking grain.

Working Properties: Easy to work with hand tools, very easy with power tools. Excellent for gluing and finishing.

Common Uses: Furniture, especially contemporary "blond" pieces.

PURPLEHEART

Other Common Names: Amaranth, Violet wood

Sources: Central America, South America

Specific Gravity: 0.67

Mechanical Properties: Very hard, very strong, and stable.

Physical Properties: Purple, with a fine texture and both straight and irregular grain.

Working Properties: Straight-grained wood is easy to work with hand tools, difficult with power tools because resin builds up on the cutting edges. Poor for gluing, good for finishing, although the oils in the wood may react with some oil-based finishes.

Common Uses: Furniture, boats, inlay, veneer, outdoor furniture.

Comments: Resists decay, potentially toxic.

ROSEWOOD, BRAZILIAN

Other Common Name: Jacaranda

Sources: South America

Specific Gravity: 0.80

Mechanical Properties: Very hard, very strong, very stable.

Physical Properties: Streaked dark brown and red-brown, with a medium-fine texture and both straight and curly grain.

Working Properties: Very difficult to work with hand tools because of its hardness and curly grain. Difficult to work with power tools because pitch builds up on the cutters. Poor for gluing, good for finishing, although the wood oils may react with some oil-based finishes.

Common Uses: Furniture, turnings, handles, veneer.

Comments: Endangered. Resists decay, potentially toxic.

2-17 Soon after European colonists discovered genuine mahogany, it became an important furniture wood. This was not just because of its elegant appearance. Mahogany was extremely well suited to the hand tool techniques that were prevalent before the Industrial Revolution. The colonists could work much faster in mahogany than in oak or other hardwoods, and could make more money. Ambitious, high-dollar cabinetmakers on both sides of the Atlantic used it to make stylish furniture during the eighteenth and early nineteenth centuries. This kneehole desk, built and carved from genuine mahogany by Edmund Townsend in 1754, is revered as one of the best examples of American Chippendale furniture. *Photo courtesy of Israel Sack, Inc.*

ROSEWOOD, INDIAN

Other Common Names: None
Sources: India, Indonesia
Specific Gravity: 0.75
Mechanical Properties: Very hard, very strong, and very stable.
Physical Properties: Streaked dark brown and purple, with a medium texture and both straight and irregular grain.
Working Properties: Difficult to work with hand tools and power tools, owing to its hardness and the oils in the wood. Poor for gluing, good for finishing, although the wood oils may react with some oil-based finishes.
Common Uses: Furniture, inlay, musical instruments, veneer.
Comments: Endangered. Resists decay, potentially toxic.

TEAK

Other Common Names: Kyun, Teka
Sources: Southeast Asia, Indonesia

2-18 From the sublime to the ridiculous — this whirligig was also made from genuine mahogany. This wood is excellent for carving. It's also highly resistant to decay, making it a good choice for outdoor projects.

Specific Gravity: 0.55
Mechanical Properties: Hard, very strong, and stable.
Physical Properties: Dark brown, with a coarse texture and both straight and irregular grain.
Working Properties: Easy to work with hand tools and power tools, provided the cutting edges are very sharp. Poor for gluing, good for finishing, although the wood oils may react with some oil-based finishes.
Common Uses: Furniture, boats, outdoor furniture, turnings, veneer.
Comments: Endangered. Decay resistant, potentially toxic.

WENGE

Other Common Name: Panga panga
Sources: Africa
Specific Gravity: Not available
Mechanical Properties: Very hard, strong, and stable.
Physical Properties: Color is dark brown, almost black. Has a coarse texture and a straight grain.
Working Properties: Easy to work with hand tools and power tools, as long as the cutting edges are sharp. Good for gluing, excellent for finishing.
Common Uses: Carving, inlay, turning. Can be used as a substitute for ebony.
Comments: Good for carving.

WORKING WITH IMPORTED WOODS

Many imported woods, particularly those from wet environments, are loaded with natural oils. These sometimes make it difficult to get a good glue bond. The oils may also react with oil-based finishes, preventing them from drying properly. There are, however, a few tricks you can use to glue and finish these woods.

When gluing an oily wood, assemble the joint as soon as you can after cutting and fitting the parts. If you let it sit for a few days — or even a few hours — the oils react with the air, making it more difficult to get a strong bond. Also, clean the wood surface with alcohol or methanol just before applying the glue — this removes some of the oils close to the surface. For the best possible bond, use epoxy cement. Of all the adhesives, this is the least affected by wood oils.

When finishing an oily wood, apply a "wash coat" of shellac and let it dry thoroughly before applying the finish. This seals the oils in the wood and prevents them from reacting with the finish. If you're mixing up the shellac from flakes, a 1-pound cut is about right. If you're using it from a can, dilute it one-to-one with denatured alcohol for the appropriate mix.

3

BUYING AND PREPARING LUMBER

Lumber is *sawed* from a tree — the round trunk is reduced to rectangular boards in a process known as *sawyering*. In today's industrialized lumber industry, sawyering has become a complex manufacturing endeavor that requires the efforts of many specialists. The head sawyer decides how a log should be sliced to get the highest possible quantity and quality of lumber. The kiln operator determines the schedule by which the green lumber is dried, removing the moisture quickly enough to turn a profit but not so quickly that it distorts the wood. The grader inspects the dried lumber and sorts it into various grades, depending on the usable wood in each board.

To get the best lumber for your money, you should understand these processes and how these professionals make their decisions along the way.

TURNING TREES INTO LUMBER

A SHORT HISTORY OF SAWYERING

Although craftsmen have been building furniture and other useful items from wood for over 5,000 years, lumber is a fairly recent development. Boards were either hand-sawed or *riven* (split) from logs until the first water-powered sawmill was built in Germany in 1321.

It's impossible to overestimate the effect that the sawmill had on woodworking. Can you imagine how little you'd get done if, every time you wanted to build something, you had to split a log from end to end, then work the riven boards down to the necessary thickness with a hand plane? Sawmills made boards affordable. Before the fourteenth century, only rich folks had wooden furniture, and most of that was pretty crude. But by the time America was settled, all but the poorest homes were furnished, and furniture making had developed into a respected craft.

Woodworking took another quantum leap forward around 1800, in the Shaker religious community at Watervliet, New York. According to legend, Sister Tabatha Babbit sat at her spinning wheel, looking out the window at two Shaker brothers as they bucked firewood with a two-man saw. She marveled at how much more efficient her revolving wheel was than their reciprocating saw. Why couldn't the brothers mount saw teeth on a wheel? At her suggestion, the

Shakers snipped a crude circular saw from tin and found that it worked. By 1808 there was a profitable sawmill at Watervliet, cutting up lumber for siding and flooring with a circular *buzz saw*.

The buzz saw remained the standard of the lumber industry until the mid-twentieth century, when band saws begin to replace the old circular saws. Today, band sawmills come in all sizes, from one-man mills no bigger than an ordinary band saw to giant computer-controlled mills with 10- and 12-inch-wide blades.

MILLING THE LOGS

In a large commercial sawmill, the logs are processed through several different saws and cutters that turn them into lumber. The first step is the *debarker,* which chews the bark off the logs. Then they're sent through a *metal detector* to sort out logs with bits of metal hidden inside them, since a single spike can ruin a mill blade. (*SEE FIGURE 3-1.*) From here, they are loaded onto the log carriage, which feeds them past the *head saw,* making the first cuts. (*SEE FIGURE 3-2.*)

If a log is to be plain-sawn or live-sawn, the first cut is a *slab cut,* removing part of the round surface and giving the log a flat side. If it's to be quarter-sawn, the

***3-1** **The first step in any milling** operation is to remove the bark from the log. The bark harbors insects, fungi, and microbes that might attack the wood if it were left attached.*

After a *debarker* chews off the bark, the log passes through a *metal detector.* Often there are old nails, fence staples, or barbed wire buried deep within the log. These can nick

the mill blade or even break it. A log found to have metal is set aside until the mill crew can locate the hazard with hand-held detectors and chop it out.

log is cut into quarters, or *bolts*. After making the initial cuts, the sawyer begins to slice boards from the log or the bolts. At a small mill, all the boards are cut at the head saw. At larger operations, the slabbed logs or bolts are sent to a *resaw* where they are sliced into boards. *(SEE FIGURE 3-3.)* **Note:** Refer to "Wood Grain" on page 3 for an explanation of plain-sawn, live-sawn, and quarter-sawn lumber.

The boards are cut to various thicknesses. The old buzz saws could be adjusted in quarter-inches — each quarter-inch was a numbered notch on the controls. To this day, wood thickness is still measured in *quarters* — 4/4, 5/4, 8/4, 12/4, and so on. To figure out how many inches thick a board is, just divide the

numbers. For example, 8/4 wood is 2 inches thick — 8 ÷ 4 = 2. **Note:** Some of the larger mills that do business overseas also cut lumber in millimeters.

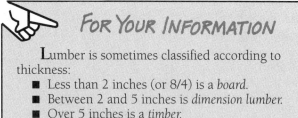

FOR YOUR INFORMATION

Lumber is sometimes classified according to thickness:
- Less than 2 inches (or 8/4) is a *board.*
- Between 2 and 5 inches is *dimension lumber.*
- Over 5 inches is a *timber.*

3-2 Once the crew is sure a log is free of bark and metal, they load it on the *log deck.* The log deck conveys the log to the *carriage,* which feeds it into the *head saw.* Here, the sawyer slabs the log (cuts one or more straight surfaces) or quarters it (cuts it into four parts or *bolts*). Pneumatic *dogs* on the carriage automatically turn the log, and a laser beam helps the sawyer align it for each cut.

3-3 From the head saw, the slabbed logs or bolts are sent to the *resaw.* The resaw slices a single board from the log, then drops it onto a *carousel.* This carries the log back around to the resaw and sends it through again, cutting another board. The process continues until nothing valuable remains of the log.

The green boards go to an *edger saw* which puts a straight edge on them, then to a *trimmer saw,* where they are cut to length. (*See Figure 3-4.*) All the bark, slabs, and trimmings are saved. Bark is usually shredded to make mulch, while slabs and trimmings are chipped to make particleboard or paper. Some mills burn the chips to provide the heat needed to dry the wood.

DRYING THE LUMBER

After lumber is milled, it's dried. The boards are stacked with evenly spaced *stickers* (narrow sticks) between them to allow the air to circulate on all sides. The stacks are *seasoned,* resting outdoors for a month or two, until the wood loses most of its free water. (*See Figure 3-5.*)

3-4 The green boards are sent to an *edger saw* (1), which rips straight edges. Here again, the operator relies on a laser beam to align each board for the rip cut. Next, the board goes to a *trimmer saw* (2), where it's cut to a standard length. (Standard lengths are usually multiples of 2 feet — 8 feet, 10 feet, 12 feet, and so on.) The final stop in the mill is the *grading station* (3). Here, someone with a trained eye inspects each board and assigns a preliminary grade based on industry standards.

3-5 The green boards are stacked with *stickers* between each layer to allow air to circulate on all sides. The positions of these stickers are critical — they must be aligned vertically. If they are placed haphazardly, the boards will dry with crooks and bows. Once stacked, the ends of the boards are sealed with paint — this keeps the ends from drying too fast and reduces end checks and splits. The stacks dry outdoors, *seasoning* until most of the free water has evaporated. This can take several weeks to several months, depending on the wood species and time of year.

Afterward, the boards may be covered or restacked in a sheltered area to *air dry*. With time, the wood loses most of its bound water, eventually reaching a moisture content more or less at rest with the prevailing relative humidity in the area. Complete air drying can take a year or more, so most commercial lumber is *kiln-dried* instead. The wood is stacked in an oven and, over the course of one to four weeks (depending on the species), reduced to an acceptable moisture content. (*See Figure 3-6.*)

This must be done carefully according to a rigid *drying schedule*. If the wood is dried too fast, it will *case harden* and check on the surface. A case-hardened board has internal stresses that cause it to cup when you plane or resaw it. In severe cases, it will *honeycomb,* checking on the inside. (*See Figure 3-7.*) If the wood isn't dried long enough, the moisture content may not be consistent and the board may warp. What's more, partially dried softwoods retain pockets of sap that ooze or bleed out of the wood.

After the wood is dried, the individual boards are inspected and given a final grade. They are also quantified according to the number of *board feet* they contain. A board foot is 144 cubic inches of wood — 1 inch by 12 inches by 12 inches. For example, an 8/4 board 12 inches wide and 8 feet long contains 16 board feet. Lumber is usually sold by the board foot.

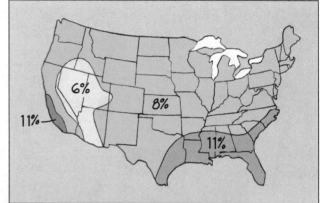

3-6 After they are seasoned, the stacks are moved to a *kiln* — a large oven. They are baked at a low temperature (between 110 and 180 degrees Fahrenheit) for a week or more to remove enough bound water to reduce the wood to a stable moisture content. In most parts of the United States, wood is kiln-dried to approximately 8 percent moisture content, but it may be as high as 11 percent in humid areas of the South, and as low as 6 percent in dry regions of the Southwest.

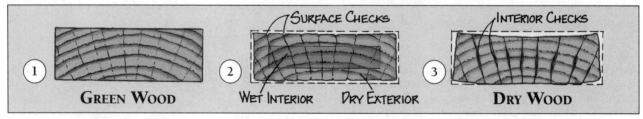

3-7 The wood fibers in a green board are saturated with moisture all the way through, and the stresses inside the board are relatively even (1). As the board starts to dry, it loses moisture near the surface first. If the moisture evaporates quickly, the wood on the outside shrinks too fast, developing surface checks in a condition called *case hardening* (2). In severe cases, the board's hardened outside prevents the inside from shrinking normally, causing interior checks or *honeycomb* (3).

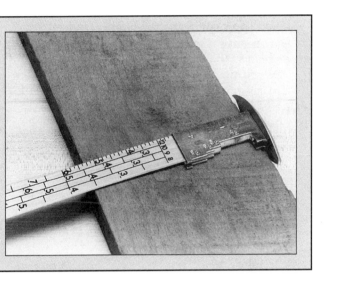

AIR DRYING VERSUS KILN DRYING

There is a common misconception among wood-workers that kiln-dried lumber is more stable than air-dried. This is not so. Every sawyer I've ever talked to has told me that it's often the other way around.

The technology of kiln-drying developed because air-drying methods couldn't keep up with demands of the furniture and construction industries. Kiln-drying not only dries wood quickly, it also sets the pitch in resinous woods, kills insects and bacteria that cause the wood to decay, and produces a more consistent moisture content than air-drying.

But kiln-drying can stress the lumber slightly. If the wood loses its bound water slowly through air-drying, the chances are it will develop fewer internal stresses. This, in turn, makes it more stable.

In certain species, air-drying also produces more vivid colors. The prevalent method for kiln-drying cherry and walnut is to heat them with steam. The steam partially dissolves the extractives in the heart-wood, creating a stain which dyes the sapwood to match. While this produces more usable lumber with less waste, it also makes the wood look flat and washed out.

You'll get wood that's more stable and possibly better looking if you look around for air-dried lumber. Unfortunately, there's very little of it available commercially — even the smallest mills kiln-dry their lumber — and you may have to dry it yourself.

CUTTING AND DRYING YOUR OWN LUMBER

Many craftsmen cut and dry their own lumber, not just to save money, but to make sure they get exactly what they want. You don't need a sawmill or a woodlot to do this — just a dry place to stack a small quantity of lumber.

If you have your own trees to cut up, fell them during the autumn or winter when they aren't full of sap. The lumber will take less time to dry and it won't be as susceptible to molds and bacteria. Take the logs to a small mill that does custom cutting and have them sawed. Or, have the sawyer come to you. Many small lumber operations have portable band sawmills that can be set up almost anywhere. (*SEE FIGURE 3-8.*) If you don't have your own trees, you can often purchase individual logs from a mill and have them cut to order.

Should you want to saw the lumber yourself, there are several ways to do this without investing in a sawmill. You can purchase a guide for a chain saw that lets you rip a log into boards where it lies. There are also gasoline-powered band saws that will do the same thing. (SEE FIGURE 3-9.) Or, if you have an ordinary band saw with a large capacity, you can use it to resaw short logs. (See the "Workshop Sawmill" on page 52.) Whatever method you use, remember to remove the bark, either by peeling the logs before you saw them or by edging the boards after they're sawed.

WHERE TO FIND IT

For information on portable chain saw mills, write:

Grandberg International
200 South Garrard Boulevard
Richmond, CA 94801

To learn more about portable band saw mills, contact:

Better Built Corporation
845 Woburn Street
Wilmington, MA 01887

3-8 Many small lumbering services have portable sawmills like the one shown. It's mounted on a trailer so it can be towed to a remote site and set up next to the tree you want sawed. Consult the sawyer before you fell the tree — many of them like to inspect the tree where it stands to make sure it's not part of an old fence row that might be imbedded with nails or wire.

3-9 This lightweight band saw is powered by a small gasoline motor, similar to a chain saw motor. This combination enables you to cut lumber from a tree where you fell it. The band saw has an adjustable guide that rides along a flat surface, letting you slab a log, then cut boards from it. Chain saw mills work in a similar manner, but the guidance system attaches to the bar of the chain saw. Cutting your own lumber in this manner is long, hard work, but both tools make it possible to plain-saw, quarter-saw, and live-saw your lumber. *Photo courtesy of Better Built Corporation, Wilmington, Massachusetts.*

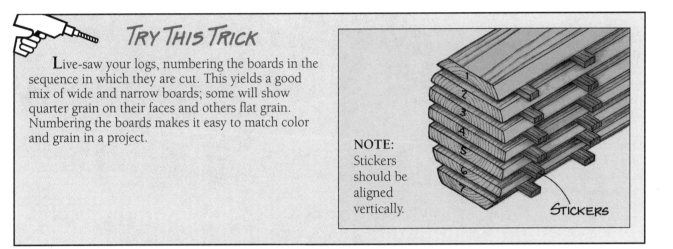

TRY THIS TRICK

Live-saw your logs, numbering the boards in the sequence in which they are cut. This yields a good mix of wide and narrow boards; some will show quarter grain on their faces and others flat grain. Numbering the boards makes it easy to match color and grain in a project.

NOTE: Stickers should be aligned vertically.

STICKERS

To dry your green lumber, make an outdoor rack large enough to accommodate the stack and high enough to hold the wood a foot or so off the ground. Stack the boards on the rack, placing stickers between each layer. Paint the ends of the boards, then cover the stack to keep most of the rain off. (*SEE FIGURES 3-10 AND 3-11.*) Also protect the stack from direct sunlight and strong winds.

Let the stack season outdoors for three to four months, during a time of year when the average temperature is above freezing. This is long enough for the free water to evaporate from most species. Then move the stack to a sheltered (but *unheated*) location inside a barn, storage shed, or garage to remove bound water and let the wood stabilize. You can use the wood when the moisture content drops below 12 percent.

How long does this take? The rule of thumb is that wood should dry one year for every inch of thickness. However, many species dry faster than this; a few, slower. To test the moisture content of your lumber,

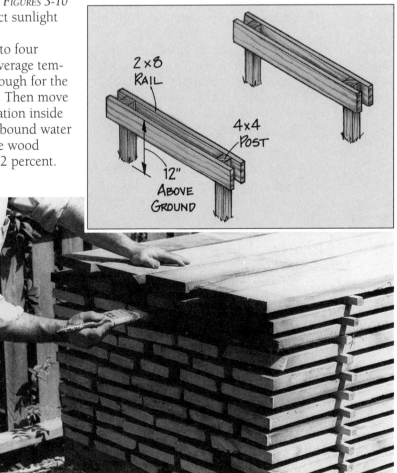

3-10 To air-dry lumber, first build a simple rack to hold the lumber about 12 inches above the ground. Space the racks every 24 inches to adequately support the wood. Stack the wood on the rack with a little space in between each board. Place *stickers* between each layer of boards, arranging the stickers so they are vertically aligned. This will provide even support and allow air to circulate around all sides of the wood. Paint the ends of the boards to prevent them from drying out faster than the centers.

3-11 Put a final layer of stickers on top of the stack, then cover the wood and the stickers with a sheet of exterior plywood. The sheet should be large enough to keep most of the rain off the stack and protect it from direct sunlight. Weight the plywood down with concrete blocks. Not only does this keep the cover from blowing away, it prevents the top layers of boards from cupping. If you live in a windy area, position a second piece of plywood on the windward side of the stack. This will serve as a baffle, preventing the breeze from blowing through the stack and drying the wood too quickly. **Note:** Do *not* cover the stack with a tarp. This will trap the moisture and the wood will mold.

purchase a *moisture meter.* Or, cut a small piece of wood from the *center* of a board in the stack. (*Don't* take it from the ends.) Carefully weigh the sample on a postage scale, then bake it in an oven at 200°F for two to three hours to remove all the remaining moisture. Weigh the sample again immediately after removing it from the oven. Subtract the oven-dried weight (DW) from the original weight (W) and divide the result by the original weight. Finally, multiply by 100 to find the moisture content (MC). Here's the equation:

$$[(W - DW) \div W] \times 100 = MC$$

For example, if the sample weighs 4 ounces before it's dried in the oven and 3½ ounces afterward, the moisture content is 12½ percent — [(4 - 3½) ÷ 4] × 100 = 12½.

Don't think that the air-dried wood will always be slightly "wetter" than kiln-dried. After a year or two, a project made from air-dried lumber will drop to the same average moisture content as kiln-dried lumber. Nor should you assume that kiln-dried lumber will always be under more stress than air-dried. After a few years, the small amount of stress accumulated by wood that has been properly kiln-dried will dissipate. Unless the kiln-dried wood has been steamed, the two types of lumber should look and act exactly the same.

SELECTING LUMBER

LUMBER GRADES

Once the wood is dried, it's classified as either yard lumber, structural lumber, or factory and shop lumber. Yard and structural lumber are used for building and construction; factory and shop lumber are what craftsmen generally buy to make furniture and other projects. Grading involves inspecting each board and scoring it according to the number of defects such as knots, splits, and shakes. The fewer defects there are, the higher the grade.

Hardwoods and softwoods are graded differently. Hardwoods are assigned *cutting grades* based on the amount of clear wood (with no defects) that can be cut from the boards. The grader looks at the board, imagining rectangular shapes that can be cut from it. Rectangular shapes with no defects in them are known as *clear face cuttings.* Those with defects are *waste. (See Figure 3-12.)* The amount of waste and the size of the clear face cuttings determine the grade of the board:

■ *Firsts and Seconds* (FAS) is the best grade. It can have no more than 16 percent waste (as scored on the *worst* side of the board) and the clear cuttings must be no smaller than 3 inches wide and 7 feet long, or 4 inches wide and 5 feet long. The boards themselves must be at least 6 inches wide and 8 feet long.

■ *FAS 1-Face* is similar to First and Seconds, but it's scored on the *best* side of the board.

■ *Selects* are similar to Firsts and Seconds, but the

boards can be smaller — as narrow as 4 inches overall and as short as 6 feet.

■ *Number 1 Common* or *Thrift* lumber can have up to 33 percent waste. The clear cuttings must be no smaller than 4 inches wide and 2 feet long, or 3 inches wide and 3 feet long. The boards must be at least 3 inches wide and 4 feet long.

There are grades with even more waste — *Number 2* and *Number 3*. But these are rarely used in furniture-making and are not commonly available.

There are also exceptions for certain species and lumber types. For example, walnut, butternut, and quarter-sawn woods can be as narrow as 5 inches overall to be classified FAS. Poplar over 8 inches wide must contain no less than 66 percent heartwood to be considered FAS. If you do a lot of work with a certain species, you should know if any special rules apply. You can find these in the National Hardwoods Lumber Association's *Hardwood Grading Rule Book.*

Softwood is graded for *appearance,* by inspecting the best face of the board. There are three grades, and several categories within each grade (*SEE FIGURE 3-13*):

■ The *Select* grades are the best softwood boards. *C and Better Select* is the clearest softwood available. It may contain small spots of torn grain, fine checks, or pitch. *D Select* may have some sound defects such as small, tight knots. *Molding Stock* offers long, clear (but narrow) rippings useful for making moldings.

■ The *Common* grades are utility wood. *Number 2 and Better Common* may have many tight knots, while *Number 3 Common* can have a single defect such as a loose knot or a knot hole.

3-12 Hardwood is graded for the amount of usable wood in each board, with the grader envisioning rectangles of usable wood that can be sawed from it by cutting around the defects. These rectangles are known as *clear face cuttings;* the remainder is *waste.* The usable rectangles must be a certain minimal size depending on the dimensions of the board. A board must be at least 6 inches wide, 8 feet long, and contain no more than 16 percent waste to be graded *Firsts and Seconds* or *FAS.* If it's narrower or shorter than that and still has no more than 16 percent waste, it's considered *Select*). And if it has up to 33 percent waste, it's *Number 1 Common* or *Thrift.*

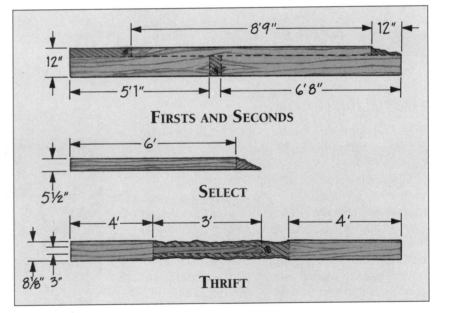

FIRSTS AND SECONDS

SELECT

THRIFT

3-13 Softwood is graded for appearance. The grader inspects the best side of the board for tight knots, loose knots, and other defects. If the board is mostly clear with just a few small, tight knots, it's considered *Select.* If it has several tight knots and no more than one loose knot or other defect, it's *Common.* If it has several loose knots but offers usable cuttings, it's *Shop.* Within each of these grades, there are several sub-categories.

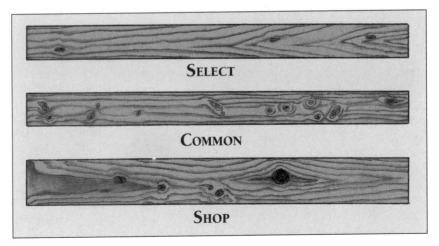

SELECT

COMMON

SHOP

■ *Shop* grades may have several defects. *Number 3 Clear* softwood must yield at least 70 percent clear cuttings — only 30 percent can be waste. *Number 1 Shop* must yield only 50 percent clear cuttings, and *Number 2 Shop* only 33 percent.

Softwood that's 5/4 and thicker is scored a little differently than wood that's 4/4 and thinner, and the rules vary somewhat for different softwood species. But the grades remain the same.

☞ WHERE TO FIND IT

You can purchase the *Hardwood Grading Rule Book* from:

National Hardwood Lumber Association
P.O. Box 34518
Memphis, TN 38184

The NHLA is also an excellent source of information on other aspects of the hardwood industry.

PURCHASING LUMBER

When you purchase lumber, you must decide what grade you want, the thicknesses you need, and the number of board feet required.

Often, the grade is the least of your worries — in most cases, it's decided for you. Many wood retailers have only one grade of hardwood available (usually FAS), others mix Selects with FAS and call it *Selects and Better.* Any of the three grades of softwoods may be available at building supply centers, but they are not necessarily labeled as such. The Selects are usually sorted out, but you frequently find Common and Shop grades mixed. The result of all this confusion is that you have to sort through the bins, choosing individual boards you think you can use, regardless of their grade.

As you sort through the boards, discard those with defects that will increase the amount of wastage or detract from your project — checks, knots, chipped grain, sapwood, stains, and so on. And pay careful attention to the wood grain. Straight grain works easily, but it's visually uninteresting. If you buy a range of grain patterns, you'll have more choices when it comes time to lay out the parts of a project.

Thickness depends on whether you're buying *rough-cut* lumber that you will plane yourself or *surfaced* lumber that's already been planed. (*See Figure 3-14.*) Rough-cut lumber should be at least ⅛ inch

thicker than you need, to allow room for planing. If you need ⅞-inch-thick wood, for instance, purchase 4/4 (1-inch-thick) rough-cut stock. When buying surfaced lumber, have it planed about ¹⁄₁₆ inch oversize. For example, if you need ¾-inch-thick wood, have the rough-cut boards planed to ¹³⁄₁₆ inch and plan on taking the last ¹⁄₁₆ inch off yourself.

Never buy wood planed to the precise thickness you need. Remember, even though the lumber has been dried, it will expand and contract because the relative humidity in your shop will be different from the humidity at the lumberyard.

To figure the number of board feet (BF) you need, consult the cutting list for your project. Sort the list by thickness to determine what rough-cut thickness you'll need. (For example, you'll need 4/4 stock to make ¾-inch-thick parts.) Multiply the widths and lengths (in inches) of each part — this will give you the *surface area* (SA) in square inches. Total the surface areas of those parts that are the same thickness and convert this figure to square feet by dividing by 144. Then multiply by the thickness of the rough-cut lumber in quarters (X/4). Here's the equation:

$$(SA \div 144) \times X/4 = BF$$

3-14 Many hardwood outlets sell wood that has been planed on both faces, known as *surfaced-two-sides* or *S2S* (*bottom*). It's tempting to buy ready-planed lumber because you can see what you're buying and it saves you some work. However, *rough-cut lumber* (*top*), boards that haven't been planed, is the better buy. You can't true a surfaced board if it cups or bows. Because it's already cut close to its final thickness, there isn't enough stock to joint it. But rough-cut lumber provides the extra stock you need for straightening and flattening.

If the ¾-inch-thick parts in your project tally 1656 inches total surface area, you'll need a *minimum* of 11½ board feet — (1656 ÷ 144) × 4/4 = 11½.

This probably won't be enough, however, because there will be some waste. If you're working with top-grade lumber, add another 10 percent for waste. (Multiply the minimum number of board feet by 1.1.) If you're working with poorer grades, add 20 or 30 percent (multiplying by 1.2 or 1.3). In our example, if you are buying Select grade (second-best) 4/4 hardwood, you'll need about 14 board feet — 11½ x 1.2 = 13.8. Round that up to 14.

PREPARING THE LUMBER

As it comes to you straight from the yard or the store, lumber is *not* ready to use. Remember, the relative humidity of your shop is almost certainly different from that of the lumberyard. When you bring the wood home, it will be in motion, either expanding or contracting. Give it two or three weeks to *shop dry*, letting it stabilize in its new environment. *This is extremely important!* If you use it right away, the joints you cut today may not fit tomorrow.

Once the wood has shop dried, select the boards you want to use. Plan how you will cut them to make the parts of your project, then lay out the parts. As you measure and mark each piece, leave yourself some extra stock, making the parts 1 to 2 inches longer and about ½ inch wider than their final

A SAFETY REMINDER

Don't bust down the lumber into pieces smaller than you can joint or plane safely. If a project requires small parts, group these together on a section of a board and cut the section free.

dimensions. Cut the boards as you've marked them, roughing out the parts. Cutting slightly oversize relieves the interior stresses in the wood before you reduce the parts to their final sizes. Craftsmen sometimes refer to this as *busting down* the lumber.

If you're working with surfaced lumber, plane the wood to its final thickness. If the board isn't quite flat or straight, there's little remedy for it — planing won't remove the distortion. All you can do is choose the flattest, straightest sections of the boards for those parts that need to be true. After planing to thickness, joint an edge straight and rip it to width. Finally, cut it to length.

This procedure is a little different for rough-cut lumber. If the wood has distorted, you can true it with some judicious jointing and planing. For each part, joint one face flat, then joint an edge square to the trued face. Plane the second face parallel to the first, rip the part to width, and cut it to length. (*SEE FIGURE 3-15.*)

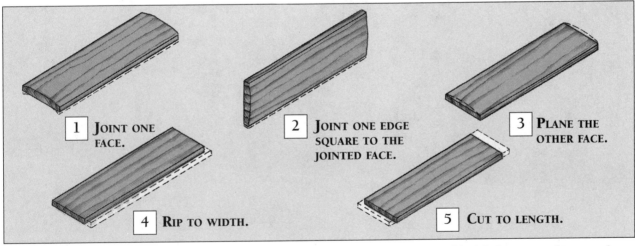

3-15 To prepare a rough-cut board, first bust it down into slightly oversize parts. (1) Joint one face of each part flat and true. (2) Turn the board on edge so the true face is against the jointer fence, then joint an edge straight and square to the face. (3) Plane the other face parallel to the jointed face, reducing the stock to its final thickness. (4) Cut the other edge parallel to the jointed edge, reducing the stock to its final width. (5) Cut one end square, then the other, reducing the board to its final length. **Note:** Some craftsmen prefer to rip the part about ¹⁄₃₂ inch wide, then joint it to its final width.

WORKSHOP SAWMILL

Have you ever run across a small log that you thought would make better lumber than firewood? If you have a band saw, you can slice small logs into usable boards by resawing them. To do this, you need a *carriage* to hold the logs and a long *support table* to support and guide the carriage as you feed the logs past the blade.

The carriage cradles the log. *Dogs* with metal points secure the log and keep it from rolling. A *guide rail* on the bottom of the carriage rides along the outside edge of the support table, guiding the log in a straight line as it's cut.

The support table fits around the band saw table and bolts to it. Folding legs brace the ends of the table, keeping it level. The entire fixture knocks down for easy storage when you aren't sawing logs.

1 **Place the log in the carriage** and adjust the dogs to hold it so about 15 percent of the log's diameter overhangs the inside edge of the car- riage base. This is the portion of the log that will be sliced off. For example, if you're sawing a log 8 inches in diameter, you want to cut off a slab about 1¼ inches thick, so the log should overhang about 1¼ inches. Secure the dogs so the log won't roll in the carriage.

2 Place the carriage on the

support table so the guide rail hooks over the outside edge. Turn on the saw and slide the carriage forward, feeding the log into the blade. As you cut, keep the rail firmly against the table's edge. This will create one flat side on the log. **Note:** Use a wide skip-tooth or hook-tooth blade for this operation.

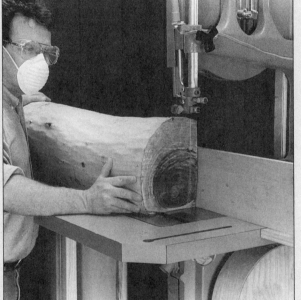

3 Turn the log 90 degrees on

the carriage so the flat side faces down. Again, position the log to cut away about 15 percent of the diameter. Secure the log and cut a second slab, creating another flat side square to the first. Repeat this process for each of the logs you want to saw up.

4 Cut at least two flat sides

90 degrees apart on all the logs. This will give you one flat side to rest on the table and another to guide along a fence. Set the log carriage aside and attach a resawing fence to the band saw table. Adjust the fence to cut boards to the desired thickness and resaw the logs.

(continued) ▷

WORKSHOP SAWMILL — CONTINUED

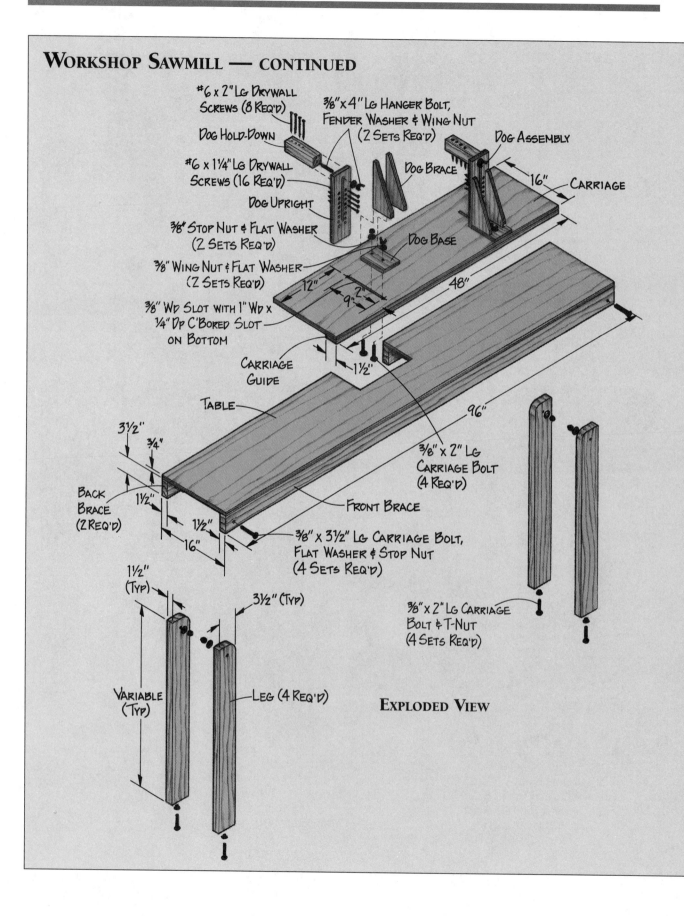

#6 x 2" Lg Drywall Screws (8 Req'd)

Dog Hold-Down

#6 x 1¼" Lg Drywall Screws (16 Req'd)

Dog Upright

⅜" Stop Nut & Flat Washer (2 Sets Req'd)

⅜" Wing Nut & Flat Washer (2 Sets Req'd)

⅜" Wd Slot with 1" Wd x ¼" Dp C'Bored Slot on Bottom

Carriage Guide

Table

⅜" x 4" Lg Hanger Bolt, Fender Washer & Wing Nut (2 Sets Req'd)

Dog Brace

Dog Assembly

16"

Carriage

Dog Base

12"

9"

2"

48"

1½"

96"

⅜" x 2" Lg Carriage Bolt (4 Req'd)

3½"

¾"

Back Brace (2 Req'd)

1½"

1½"

16"

Front Brace

⅜" x 3½" Lg Carriage Bolt, Flat Washer & Stop Nut (4 Sets Req'd)

1½" (Typ)

3½" (Typ)

⅜" x 2" Lg Carriage Bolt & T-Nut (4 Sets Req'd)

Variable (Typ)

Leg (4 Req'd)

EXPLODED VIEW

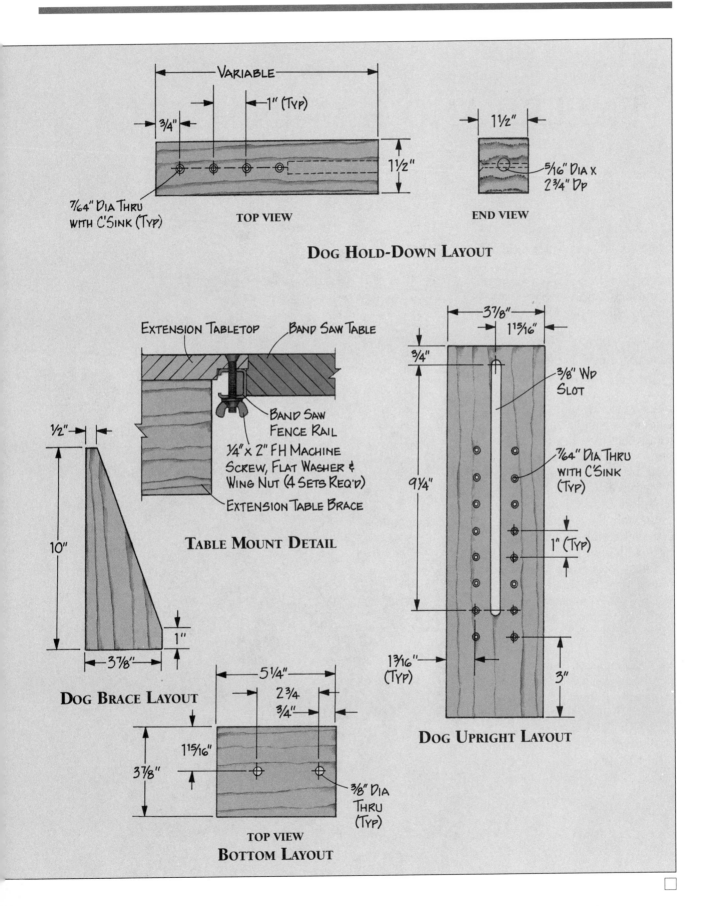

VARIABLE

1" (TYP)

3/4"

1 1/2"

7/64" DIA THRU
WITH C'SINK (TYP)

TOP VIEW

1 1/2"

5/16" DIA X
2 3/4" DP

END VIEW

DOG HOLD-DOWN LAYOUT

EXTENSION TABLETOP   BAND SAW TABLE

BAND SAW
FENCE RAIL

1/4" X 2" FH MACHINE
SCREW, FLAT WASHER &
WING NUT (4 SETS REQ'D)

EXTENSION TABLE BRACE

TABLE MOUNT DETAIL

1/2"

10"

1"

3 7/8"

DOG BRACE LAYOUT

3 7/8"

1 15/16"

1" (TYP)

5 1/4"

2 3/4

3/4"

1 15/16"

3 7/8"

3/8" DIA
THRU
(TYP)

TOP VIEW
BOTTOM LAYOUT

3 7/8"

1 15/16"

3/4"

3/8" WD
SLOT

7/64" DIA THRU
WITH C'SINK
(TYP)

9 1/4"

1" (TYP)

1 3/16"
(TYP)

3"

DOG UPRIGHT LAYOUT

4

VENEERS AND LAMINATES

Since the beginnings of woodworking, craftsmen have used *veneers* — thin slices of exceptionally beautiful woods — to dress up mundane surfaces. Archaeologists have found veneered furniture in Egyptian tombs dating back almost 5,000 years. These ancient veneers were probably split by hand, then painstakingly scraped paper-thin. Because this process was so laborious, veneering didn't become a common technique until the seventeenth century, when the invention of the *veneer saw* — a slender, fine-tooth blade in a wooden frame — made it possible to cut veneer with less effort. Much of the classic furniture from the eighteenth and early nineteenth century is decorated with sawed veneers.

Today, most veneers are sliced from a log with a huge knife, a much quicker process than sawing. And there are many new uses for them. Not only are veneers used to enhance plain surfaces, but they are also laminated to make large, flat sheets of plywood and molded shapes. Additionally, we have developed artificial veneers or *plastic laminates* made from a combination of paper and plastic resins. These are used to decorate surfaces and make them more durable.

VENEERS

TYPES OF VENEERS

Although veneers were once sawed, nowadays all but the most brittle woods are sliced. This, in fact, is the modern definition of the word — a veneer is a thin *slice* of a log or a timber.

How thin is veneer? There are several standard thicknesses, each with specific uses (*SEE FIGURE 4-1*).

■ $\frac{1}{128}$- to $\frac{1}{100}$-inch-thick slices are used to make *reinforced veneers* (also called *flexible veneers*). These superthin slices are typically bonded to sheets of paper, but they may also be stuck to cloth or plastic, depending on the application. Reinforced veneers are typically applied to tightly curved surfaces.

■ *Common veneers* are $\frac{1}{40}$ to $\frac{1}{28}$ inch thick. These either dress up flat surfaces in furniture and cabinets, or they are used as the surface veneers in plywood.

■ Veneers $\frac{1}{10}$ to $\frac{3}{16}$ inch thick make up the middle plies or the *cores* in plywood.

Although it's possible to slice wood into considerably thicker pieces, anything over $\frac{1}{4}$ inch is not considered to be a veneer. Instead, it's known as *slicewood*. Thick slices are sometimes used in the manufacture of plywood and other composite materials.

Common veneers sliced from inexpensive woods are sometimes used as *utility veneers*. These may be used under a decorative face veneer or on the back side of a veneered panel to help smooth or stabilize the surface.

MAKING VENEER

Veneer is usually sliced hot and green — high temperature and moisture content help to soften the wood fibers so the knife can make smooth cuts. Often, the logs are stored in ponds or pools to keep them from drying out, then cooked for several days prior to cutting the veneer. The mill crew checks them for metal and strips off the bark just before slicing.

There are three different methods for slicing veneer from logs (*SEE FIGURES 4-2 THROUGH 4-4*).

■ The veneer manufacturer may *flitch-cut* the logs on a *veneer slicer*. He first halves or quarters the logs, making pieces known as *flitches,* then slices the flitches straight through. Depending on how the flitch is held when it moves past the knives, the slices will show flat grain, quarter grain, or anything in between. Consequently, flitch-cut veneer looks a lot like solid wood when it's applied to a surface.

■ The manufacturer can cut logs whole on a *veneer lathe.* This machine mounts a log between centers and spins it like a large turning. As the log rotates, a knife shaves the log to produce a continuous ribbon of veneer, as wide as the log is long. As the ribbon leaves the log, it's cut into sheets. *Rotary cutting* is a fast and efficient way to produce veneer. However, because the knife makes a continuous tangential cut, rotary-cut sheets show flat grain only. This type of veneer is most commonly used for making plywood.

■ Veneer lathes can be modified for *stay-log cutting.* The manufacturer mounts the logs off-center and swings them past the knife, slicing an arc through the wood. In many cases, the logs are sawn into flitches first, then the flitches are mounted and swung. As with flitch cutting, this method produces several different grain patterns, depending on how the log or the flitch is held in relation to the knife.

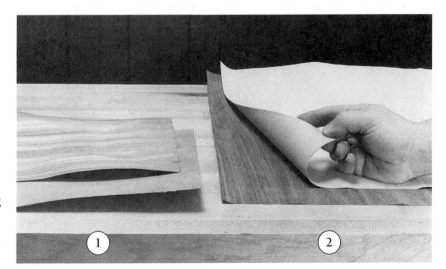

4-1 There are two types of veneer commercially available to craftsmen — *common veneer* (1), which is usually $\frac{1}{40}$ to $\frac{1}{28}$ inch thick, and *reinforced veneer* (2), which is much thinner and bonded to a backing material such as paper. Although it's easier to apply than common veneer, reinforced veneer is not as durable. It's prone to surface checks and it's very easy to sand through the thin wood layer, exposing the backing. For this reason, it's best used only for covering tight curves and other surfaces that would be difficult to cover with common veneer.

After the logs are sliced, the green veneer is dried on a hot platen (a large metal plate) or in a kiln. Unlike lumber, which can take a week or more to dry, veneer can be processed in just 10 to 20 minutes on the average. The target moisture content depends on how the veneer will be used. Veneer that will be bent or molded is dried to just 20 percent moisture content, face veneers (for plywood) to no more than 10 percent, and the commercial hardwood veneers to no more than 8 percent.

FOR YOUR INFORMATION

Flitch-cutting and stay-log cutting both produce *leaves* of veneer. (One leaf is a single slice.) Often, the leaves from a single flitch are sold together as a *book* of veneer. This enables you to match them for color and grain.

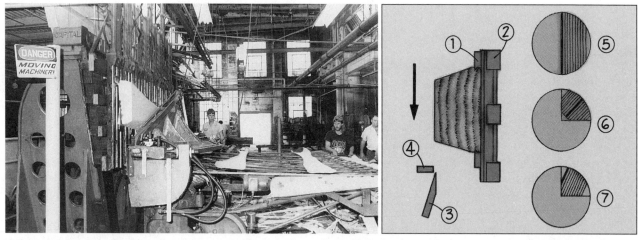

4-2 A *veneer slicer* holds a portion of a log (known as a flitch) between two sets of *dogs* (1). The dogs are mounted on a *carriage* (2). The carriage moves the flitch past a *knife* (3), slicing a narrow sheet (or leaf) of veneer. A *pressure bar* (4) presses against the flitch ahead of the knife to control splitting and checking. This process is called *flitch cutting*.

Depending on how the flitch is mounted, it can be *flat-sliced* (5), *quarter-sliced* (6), or *rift-sliced* (7). Each method produces a different grain pattern.

4-3 A *veneer lathe* mounts a whole log between two centers or *chucks* (1), then spins it. As it spins, a long *knife* (2) cuts a thin, continuous ribbon of wood. A *pressure bar* (3) presses against the log just ahead of the knife to prevent the wood from splitting or checking as it's cut. This is *rotary cutting* (4). As the rotary-cut veneer rolls off the lathe, it's chopped into sheets. Because this veneer is produced by a continuous tangential cut, all the sheets show flat grain. *Photo courtesy of Georgia-Pacific Corporation, Atlanta, Georgia.*

4-4 Stay-log cutting produces a variety of grain patterns on a veneer lathe. In this method, a log or flitch is mounted off-center. A special *eccentric chuck* (1) holds the log and swings it past the *knife* (2) and the *pressure bar* (3). Depending on how the log or flitch is mounted, it can be *half-round cut* (4), *back-cut* (5), or *rift-cut* (6).

VENEER CORE MATERIALS

The surface to which you apply the veneer is called the *core material* or the *ground*. Take care in selecting and preparing the core — it must be relatively stable and perfectly flat. If it's not stable, the core may expand and contract more than the veneer, causing the veneer to split or buckle. If it's not flat, any imperfections will "telegraph," or show through the veneer.

Hardwood plywood makes a good, strong core. Medium-density fiberboard (MDF) is a good choice, too, although it's not as strong as plywood. Particleboard is a fair choice, but it's not as smooth or stable as MDF. If you use solid wood, it should be quartersawn, showing quarter grain on the face to be veneered. Avoid plain-sawn stock and softwood plywood. Plain-sawn wood expands and contracts too much; softwood plywood is not smooth enough.

Inspect the core for dents, gouges, and other imperfections. If necessary, fill these defects with wood putty or auto body filler and sand them flush. (*SEE FIGURE 4-5.*) In some cases, you may want to apply a utility veneer to one or both faces of the core to smooth the surface, prevent it from warping, or help stabilize it. (*SEE FIGURE 4-6.*)

FOR BEST RESULTS

The veneer *and* the core to which you apply it should all "shop dry" for a week or more to make sure *all* the materials are at rest with the prevailing relative humidity in your location. If one of the materials is in motion, the veneer may buckle or split after it's applied.

4-5 The surface to which you apply the veneer must be as smooth and clean as possible — any dents, gouges, or other defects will create depressions in the finished project. Dust will keep the veneer from bonding. Fill any voids with stick shellac, wood putty, or auto body filler (*shown*). Let the filler harden completely, then sand the surface smooth. Vacuum the surface and wipe it down with a tack rag to remove all the sanding dust.

4-6 Depending on the material
you've chosen for the core, you may
want to apply an inexpensive *utility
veneer* to one or both faces. For
example, if you're veneering an
unsupported wooden surface (a
surface that's not braced or part of a
structure that will keep it from cupping), use utility veneer as *crossbanding* (1) to help stabilize the
wood. Apply a layer to both back
faces with the grain perpendicular
to the wood grain. Then apply the
decorative veneer to the front and
another layer of utility veneer to the
back. The grain of the front and back
veneers should be parallel to the
wood grain. If you're covering an
unsupported MDF or particleboard
panel, apply utility veneer to the
back surface (2). Then apply the face
veneer to the front so the grain is
parallel to that of the utility veneer.
The two veneers will balance each
other, preventing the material from
warping when the veneers expand
or contract.

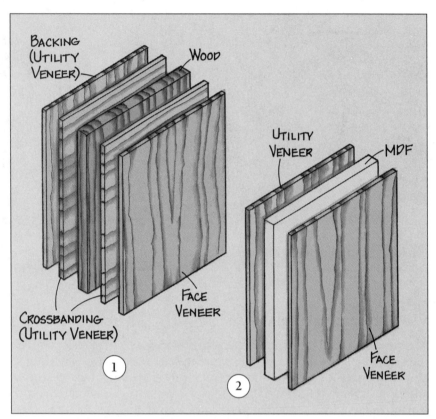

MATCHING THE VENEER

You may wish to join two or more pieces of veneer to
make a sheet large enough to cover the core, to create
a decorative effect, or both. To do this, first decide
which surface of the veneers will be exposed when
they are applied. Because of the way in which veneers
are cut, they have tiny surface checks on one face.
This is called the *loose face,* while the side without
checks is the *tight face.* Craftsmen generally prefer to
show the tight face, although some matching techniques prevent this. Inspect the veneer to identify the
tight face and mark it. (*See Figure 4-7.*)

   Next, match the pieces — that is, orient the leaves
in the way you want to join them. If you have purchased random sheets of veneer, all you can do is
make a *random match,* arranging the sheets side by
side so the wood grain and color look continuous,
just as if you were gluing boards of random widths
edge to edge. If you've purchased a "book" of veneers
and all the leaves are from the same flitch, there are
many different patterns you can create. You might
simply arrange them side by side in the order in
which they were cut, creating a *slip match.* Open the
flitch like the pages of a book, creating a *book match.*

Or, you can cut four sheets at an angle, then arrange
them so the angled wood grain forms a *diamond
match. Figure 4-8* shows several possibilities.

MOLDING VENEER

In addition to applying veneers to flat surfaces, you
can also mold them into curved shapes. *Laminate*
several layers together in a bending form, gluing the
veneers face to face. (*See Figure 4-9.*) Each veneer layer
will buttress the adjoining layers, preventing them
from unbending.

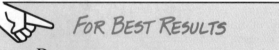

For Best Results

   Don't use water-based contact cement to
apply wood veneer. When you coat the veneer
with this adhesive, the water causes it to swell.
Unless you wait several hours for the veneer to dry
completely, it will be swollen when you bond it to
the ground. Later, when the water evaporates and
the veneer shrinks, it will split.

4-7 To find the tight face on a piece of veneer, roll the veneer parallel to the grain. If you roll it *away* from the tight face, the surface checks on the loose face will close and the veneer will seem difficult to bend. When you roll it *toward* the tight face, the checks will open up and it will be easy to bend. Once you've identified the tight face, mark it — this is the face you want to expose when you apply the veneer.

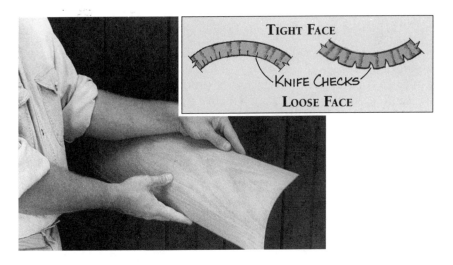

4-8 If you purchase random leaves of veneer and need to join them, make a *random match* (1), arranging them for the best effect. If the leaves are all sliced from the same log or flitch and you know the approximate order in which they were cut, you can create geometric patterns with the wood grain, such as the *slip match* (2), *book match* (3), *butt match* (4), *diamond match* (5), and *reverse diamond match* (6). You can even combine patterns, such as the *butt-and-book match* (7).

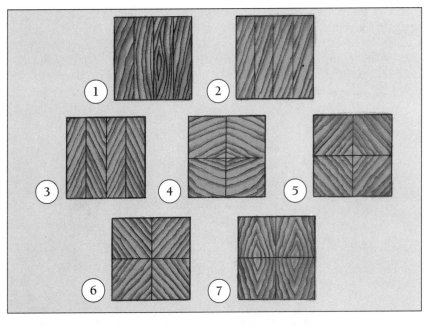

4-9 To mold veneers into a curved shape, make a *bending form* — a block of wood, plywood, or particleboard cut to the shape you want to create. Cut enough strips of veneer to bend around the curved surface of the form, and make up the desired thickness. Glue the strips face to face, bending them against the form as you do so. Clamp the strips to the form while the glue dries. Here, a *vacuum bag* serves as a clamp. When the air is evacuated from the bag, the air on the outside presses against the bag and the veneers, evenly distributing the pressure across the entire surface.

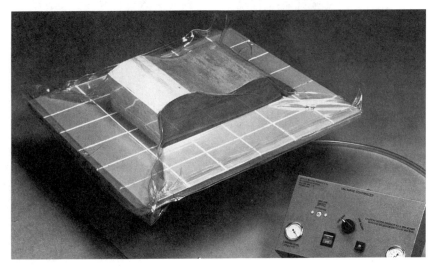

LAMINATES

Plastic laminates are durable surface treatments made by sticking together multiple layers of paper. In most laminates, the top layer of paper is colored or printed with a decorative design, although there are a few in which all the layers are the same color. The papers are bonded with a *phenol resin,* a type of plastic. This makes the laminates waterproof and highly resistant to chemicals, heat, and wear — much more so than wooden veneers. (*SEE FIGURE 4-10.*)

TYPES OF LAMINATES

There are five types of plastic laminates commonly available:

■ *General-purpose* laminate is $\frac{1}{16}$ inch thick and used for surfaces that see a good deal of wear and tear, such as the tops and edges of counters. (*SEE FIGURE 4-11.*)

■ *Vertical-surface* laminate is $\frac{1}{32}$ inch thick and used for the sides and other outside surfaces of cabinets that see less wear.

■ *Post-forming* laminate is $\frac{1}{32}$ inch thick (or thinner), and will conform to curved surfaces if warmed with a heat gun as you fit it to a project.

■ *Backing* laminate is just $\frac{1}{50}$ inch thick and does not come in colors or designs. It's sometimes applied to the back of a panel to control warping.

■ *Liner* laminate is similar to backing laminate, but it's available in either white or colors. It's designed to line the interiors of cabinets.

All of these types are available in large sheets of various sizes, 24 to 48 inches wide and up to 12 feet long. The two most common sizes are 4 feet by 8 feet and 30 inches by 10 feet.

LAMINATE CORES

Like veneers, laminates are applied to a core material. Because the laminates don't move at all, the core must be as stable as possible. The best materials are hardwood plywood and medium-density fiberboard. Particleboard is only a fair choice since it's not very strong or smooth, but it's the most common core material because it's the least expensive.

4-10 Plastic laminates are available in many different thicknesses, colors, patterns, even textures. They are made from layers of paper, bonded together by a waterproof resin. Typically, only the topmost paper is printed with the color or pattern.

4-11 Plastic laminate is much more durable than veneer. It's designed to resist water, chemicals, and extreme wear and tear. It's an excellent material for work surfaces, including those in the workshop. Both the sliding table and the table extension on this table saw are covered with plastic laminate.

5

PLYWOOD AND OTHER SHEET MATERIALS

When veneering was all the rage in the eighteenth century, craftsmen began to experiment with homemade plywood, gluing sheets of veneer face to face to make thicker panels. But plywood didn't become a popular building material until the mid-nineteenth century when John Henry Belter, a German immigrant working in New York, began to produce Victorian "Rococo" furniture from laminated veneers.

Rococo furniture was extremely elaborate, both in construction and decoration. Belter invented a method of molding layers of veneers into curved sheets and other shapes to simplify the joinery. He alternated the grain direction of each layer, making a strong, stable material that he carved into delicate shapes. In effect, Belter made the first plywood furniture.

Belter's techniques were widely imitated, and American furniture makers soon found that plywood offered another important advantage besides strength and stability. Turning trees into plywood produced larger quantities of useful building material than simply sawing them into lumber. This became increasingly important as virgin forests disappeared and sawyers began to harvest smaller, second-growth trees. By the early twentieth century, plywood was an indispensable woodworking material, commonly available in sheets of standard sizes.

Other "engineered" wood products soon followed. As manufacturing processes improved, sawyers found new ways to create large panels from smaller and smaller pieces of wood. Today, there are dozens of sheet materials made from wood particles of every size, from large chips to individual fibers. Some are designed for specific purposes and others for general construction; each of them has useful properties that you can't find in ordinary wood.

PLYWOOD

PLYWOOD CONSTRUCTION

Plywood is a laminated panel, made up of several thin layers (or *plies*) glued together face to face. (*SEE FIGURE 5-1.*) The outside plies are referred to as the *face* and the *back,* while the inside plies make up the *core.* These are glued up in broad sheets and usually trimmed to 48 inches wide and 96 inches long.

The outside layers are always wood veneer, but the inside layers may be other materials such as particleboard or solid wood. The grain direction in the veneer layers alternates — each layer is turned 90 degrees from the adjacent layers. Those layers in which the wood grain runs perpendicular to the face and back layers are *crossbands.* This arrangement restricts the movement of the assembly, preventing the wood from expanding and contracting as much as it would otherwise.

Plywood typically has an uneven number of plies — three, five, seven, and so on. This arrangement helps keep the panels flat. Laminated assemblies tend to warp or twist unless stresses caused by wood movement are properly *balanced.* The best way to balance plywood is to glue two outside plies on either side of a middle ply, making three plies in all. (The grain directions in the outside plies are parallel to one another but perpendicular to the middle.) For thicker plywood, additional plies are added in pairs to keep the assembly balanced. If, for some reason, the plywood must have an even number of plies, the grain directions in the two middle plies are parallel, making them behave as if they were one thick layer. (*SEE FIGURE 5-2.*)

Other factors affect balance. The plywood remains flatter and is more stable when all the plies are the same thickness. Even though the face veneers may be fairly thin, the veneers in the cores of the best plywoods are all the same thickness. And grain direction

5-1 Plywood veneers are usually rotary-cut, then chopped or split into sheets of specific sizes. The mill crew selects the sheets and feeds them into a press where they are sprayed with glue, laid face to face, then pressed together to make panels. The press heats the panels to help the glue cure quickly. As soon as the glue sets, the panel is released from the press and stacked horizontally until the glue hardens completely. **Note:** Although many different adhesives are used to manufacture plywood, the most common is aliphatic resin — similar to ordinary "yellow" glue. *Photos courtesy of Georgia-Pacific Corporation, Atlanta, Georgia.*

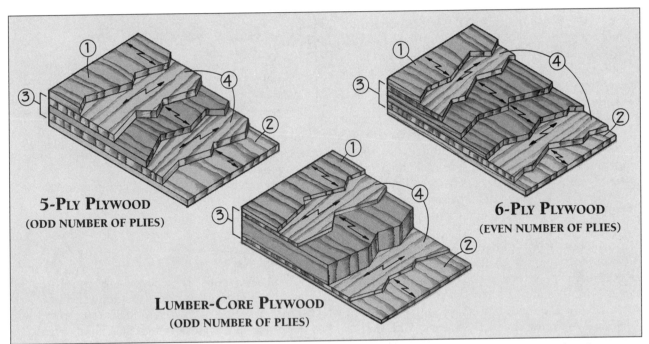

5-PLY PLYWOOD
(ODD NUMBER OF PLIES)

LUMBER-CORE PLYWOOD
(ODD NUMBER OF PLIES)

6-PLY PLYWOOD
(EVEN NUMBER OF PLIES)

5-2 Plywood is glued up from multiple layers or *plies*. Every sheet has a *face* (1) — the side with the highest quality veneer. The opposite side is the *back* (2), and the material in between is called the *core* (3). The grain direction in each ply is perpendicular to the adjacent plies, and the plies in which the grain direction runs perpendicular to the face and back are *crossbands* (4). There are usually an odd number of plies. If the plywood has an even number of plies, the wood grain in the two middle plies is oriented in the same direction so the plies move as one. If the plywood has a solid wood core, it's sandwiched between an even number of veneers, making an odd number of layers.

is critical. The wood grain in each ply must be precisely perpendicular to the adjacent plies. Furthermore, the grain direction of the odd- and even-numbered plies must be parallel to one another. If, for example, the wood grain on the back veneer is cocked at a slight angle to the face, the plywood will twist, cup, or warp.

The quality of the wood used to make the core also affects stability. Not only do knots and defects upset the balance, certain species are easier to balance than others. The best core woods are relatively stable and lightweight. It also helps if the density is consistent. Poplar, for instance, makes a good core wood. It expands and contracts less than most hardwoods, its specific gravity is only 0.42 (making it lighter than most), and there is little difference in density between the springwood and summerwood.

CHARACTERISTICS OF PLYWOOD

In addition to plywood's crossbanded construction, there are several other important differences between it and solid wood.

STABILITY

Plywood is much more stable *across its width* than solid wood. However, it's not completely stable; plywood *does* move. It expands and contracts across its thickness every bit as much as solid wood, and there is a small amount of movement along its length and width. How much movement? The amount depends on the type of plywood and material in its plies. Generally, it's slightly more than the longitudinal movement of the wood from which it's made, and ranges between 0.1 and 0.2 percent. A 48-inch-wide piece of plywood may expand and contract $\frac{1}{16}$ inch over the course of a year. (*SEE FIGURE 5-3.*)

Plywood is less susceptible to distortion than solid wood. It won't warp, bow, or cup, provided you don't disturb its balance. (If you resaw plywood or sand away one or more of the plies, it will distort.)

STRENGTH

Contrary to a popular misconception, plywood is not necessarily stronger than wood, nor is it equally strong along its length and width. The *shear strength* of plywood is much greater than wood — because of its crossbanding, plywood will not split as easily as wood. The crossbanding also helps the material distribute a load along its length *and* width. However, plywood is not as stiff as solid wood. And most plywoods are slightly stronger along the grain of the face veneer than they are across it. Plywoods with solid wood cores are much stronger in this direction.

GLUING AND FASTENING

Plywood can be glued as easily as solid wood and forms just as strong a bond. But it differs from wood in its ability to hold nails and screws. If you drive fasteners through the thickness, perpendicular to the plies, plywood will hold them better. Because of the crossbanding, it has less tendency to split — you can put the fasteners close to the edge, especially if there are many thin veneer plies. However, when you drive fasteners parallel to the plies, they don't hold as well — the plies tend to split apart. To compensate for this, use longer screws or screws designed especially for plywood. (*SEE FIGURE 5-4.*)

Note: All of these characteristics vary with the quality and the species of wood used to make the plywood, as well as the type of adhesive that holds them together.

TYPES OF PLYWOOD

There are two general categories of plywood — *construction* plywood and *decorative* or *cabinet* plywood.

TRY THIS TRICK

You can increase the holding power of screws by dipping the threads in epoxy cement before you drive them.

Construction plywood is used almost exclusively in carpentry and the building trades; most woodworkers work with cabinet plywood.

Cabinet plywood is classified according to:
- Thickness
- Core construction
- Adhesive
- Wood species

THICKNESS

Cabinet plywoods can be anywhere from ⅛ to 3 inches thick or more, but the commonly available thicknesses are ¼, ⅜, ½, and ¾ inch. You can special-order other thicknesses through most lumberyards. **Note:** These measurements are *nominal* thicknesses only. Most plywood is actually ¹⁄₃₂ inch thinner than its label would have you believe. For example, ¾-inch plywood is actually ²³⁄₃₂ inch thick.

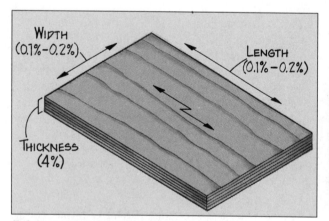

5-3 Because of the way in which it's made, plywood does not have longitudinal, tangential, or radial planes like solid woods. There is only *length* (parallel to the face grain), *width* (across the face grain), and *thickness.* Plywood is relatively stable across its length and width, but it moves as much as solid wood across its thickness.

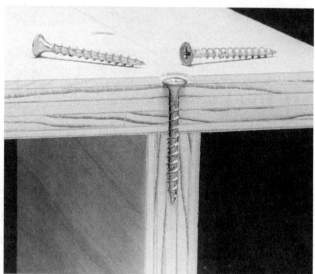

5-4 A screw driven parallel to the plies of plywood won't hold as well as one driven in solid wood. This is also true for other sheet materials — particleboard and fiberboard won't hold screws as well as wood no matter how you drive them. *Deep-thread screws* (shown) partially solve this problem. The enlarged threads have more holding power.

CORE CONSTRUCTION

There are four types of plywood cores (*SEE FIGURE 5-5*):

■ *Veneer core* plywood is the most common. It also provides the greatest stability for the least expense. Thin plywoods (¼ and ⅜ inch) usually have three veneer plies. Medium plywoods (½ and ⅝ inch) have five, while thicker plywoods (¾ and 1 inch) may have as many as seven.

■ *Lumber core* plywood is made with sawed lumber at its center. This material has many of the advantages of solid wood. It's stronger than other types of plywood, easier to cut, and offers a better edge for shaping. Despite these assets, there is a limited demand for this type of plywood and it is becoming increasingly hard to find.

■ *Fiber core* plywood has a core made from hardboard or medium-density fiberboard. Fiber-core is weak but very stable and perfectly flat.

■ *Particle core* plywood has a particleboard core. This is the weakest and least expensive type.

ADHESIVES

There are many different adhesives used to bond the plies, but they are all classified according to their *exposure capability* — their ability to resist moisture and bad weather.

■ *Exterior* plywood can be used inside or out; its plies won't fall apart in a wet environment. Plywoods made from hardwoods with exterior adhesives are sometimes labeled *Technical Type* or *Type 1.*

■ *Interior* plywoods are intended for inside use only. *Type II* hardwood plywood is made with a *moisture-resistant* adhesive. It will withstand some wetting, but will delaminate when constantly exposed to moisture. (This is the most common type of interior plywood.) *Type III* will come apart if wetted, and must be kept reasonably dry.

WOOD SPECIES

Manufacturers make plywood cores from both softwoods and hardwoods.

■ *Softwood* plywood is normally used for construction, but some of the better grades are classified as cabinet plywoods.

■ *Hardwood* plywood is generally higher in quality than softwood and is preferred for cabinetmaking and furniture making.

A wide variety of fine woods are used for face and back veneers. In hardwood plywood, maple, birch, walnut, cherry, mahogany, and oak are common. In softwood plywood, you can easily find both Douglas fir and ponderosa pine. Other species may be available by special order.

5-5 There are four types of plywood cores — *veneer core* (1), *lumber core* (2), *fiber core* (3), and *particle core* (4).

PLYWOOD GRADES

Plywood is graded with a two-character code. The first character indicates the quality of veneer face, and the second the quality of the back. (*SEE FIGURE 5-6.*) Hardwood and softwood plywoods are graded differently.

HARDWOOD PLYWOOD

The *face veneers* of domestic hardwood plywood are graded with letter codes — AA, A, B, C, D, and E. (*SEE FIGURE 5-7.*) AA is the best grade; the veneers have almost no defects and are closely matched for color and grain. A allows a few defects and slight variations in color between matched veneers. B veneers have more defects and color variations. By the time you get to C, there are streaks, stains, pin knots, and wide differences in color. Consequently, C, D, and E are considered utility grades.

The *back veneers* are graded with number codes: 1, 2, 3, and 4. Grades 1 and 2 provide smooth, sound surfaces with all large defects plugged, although there may be some tiny holes (less than ¹⁄₁₆ inch in diameter) in 2. Grades 3 and 4 permit some open defects such as splits and knotholes.

Imported hardwood plywoods are graded differently than those made in the United States. The face veneers are graded BBPF, BB, CC, and OVL, in descending order of quality. The back veneers are graded A and B, with A being the best.

SOFTWOOD PLYWOOD

Both the face and the back veneers of softwood plywood are graded with the same letter code.

5-6 Most plywood has a *grade stamp* to show the species and the quality of the face and back materials, although more and more manufacturers are using bar code *grade stickers*, as shown. Hardwood plywoods and cabinet-grade softwood plywoods are stamped or stickered on the edge to keep the veneer surfaces clean. This particular sticker tells you that the face and back are white paper birch. The face veneer

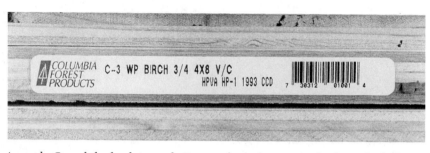

is grade C, and the back is grade 3. V/C indicates this is veneer core plywood, and the other numbers show

the industry standard to which the plywood conforms.

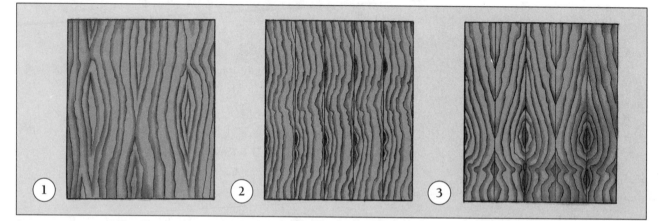

5-7 In addition to species and veneer quality, the grade stamp may also indicate how the face veneer was cut. ROT indicates a *rotary cut* (1) — the face was sliced from the log in a

continuous tangential cut. This shows unnaturally wide bands of springwood and summerwood. FLAT indicates either a flitch cut or stay-log cut, and these veneers will look

more like ordinary boards joined edge to edge. Depending on the manufacturer, flitch-cut and stay-log-cut veneers may be *slip matched* (2) or *book matched* (3).

N indicates a smooth veneer that will look good with a natural finish. The veneer pieces are all heartwood or all sapwood, carefully joined and matched. This grade is not commonly available; you may have to special-order it.

A is smooth with a few repairs. It looks okay with a natural finish, but there may be a noticeable contrast between the veneer pieces.

B has a solid surface with tight knots, repair plugs, and small splits.

C-Plugged has small, open knots and splits, but the larger defects are repaired. These repairs may be made with putty rather than wooden plugs.

C indicates medium-size open knots, splits, discoloration, and sanding defects, none of which affect the strength of the panel.

D has large knots and other defects. Because these may impair the strength of the panel, the uses of this grade are limited.

PLYWOOD GROUPS

Additionally, plywood is categorized into groups according to the strength or the specific gravity of the species used to make the core. Hardwood plywoods are divided into Groups A, B, and C, with the strongest being Group A. Softwood plywoods are divided into Groups 1 through 5. The lower the number, the stronger the plywood.

What grades and groups should you purchase? Unless you need a particularly strong or stiff plywood for a special application, you rarely need to worry about the group rating. Generally, woodworkers choose plywood for grade only. Use B-2 (B on one side and 2 on the other) or better hardwood plywood for the outside (visible parts) of furniture and cabinets, and C-2 or C-3 for the inside. When buying softwood plywood, look for N-B or A-B for the outside, and no less than B-B for the inside.

SPECIAL PLYWOODS

There are many other types of plywood you might consider for specific applications. Here are four of the most common:

■ If you plan to paint your project, consider *medium-density overlay (MDO)* plywood. This has a thin, resin-impregnated paper overlay on one or both sides and provides a perfectly smooth base for paints. It's made with an exterior adhesive and is often used for outdoor signs.

■ For a top-quality exterior cabinet-grade plywood, select *marine plywood.* This product has A- and B-grade faces, a high-quality core with no voids, and is laminated with a waterproof glue. It's designed for boat building, but can be used for many other applications.

■ Should you want to bend a sheet of plywood around a corner, there are several products designed just for this purpose. Most *bendable plywoods* have only three plies — a relatively thick face and back laminated to a thin veneer core. (*See Figure 5-8.*)

■ For an extremely strong, extremely stable plywood, purchase *European birch plywood.* (In Europe, this is referred to as *multi-ply.*) This material is made from many thin veneer layers, all of which are exactly the same thickness. (*See Figure 5-9.*) The veneers are reasonably clear, so there are very few voids. **Note:** Unlike American-made plywood, European birch comes in sheets that are approximately 60 inches square. The thicknesses are metric, but they roughly correspond to the thicknesses of domestic materials.

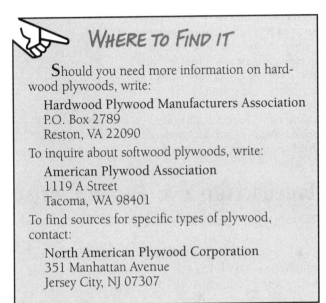

WHERE TO FIND IT

Should you need more information on hardwood plywoods, write:

Hardwood Plywood Manufacturers Association
P.O. Box 2789
Reston, VA 22090

To inquire about softwood plywoods, write:

American Plywood Association
1119 A Street
Tacoma, WA 98401

To find sources for specific types of plywood, contact:

North American Plywood Corporation
351 Manhattan Avenue
Jersey City, NJ 07307

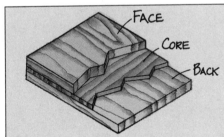

5-8 Bendable plywood is typically just ¼ to ⅜ inch thick and has just three plies — a thick face and back glued to a thin veneer core. The face and back are normally made from a "soft" hardwood with a low specific gravity, such as mahogany, lauan, or poplar. This arrangement lets you bend the plywood around a fairly sharp corner, making a curved surface on a cabinet or other piece of furniture. It's available on special order from many lumberyards under brand names such as Wiggle Wood, Bendy Board, and Italian Bending Poplar.

5-9 The strongest and most stable plywood available is *multi-ply*. Although expensive, it's an excellent material for making jigs and fixtures, such as this router table, or any other project where you need a tough, flat surface. Most multi-ply is imported from Europe and is commonly referred to as *European birch* or *Baltic birch*. (Baltic Birch is actually a brand name.) One American manufacturer makes a similar product from alder hardwood called Apple-Ply.

FIBERBOARD AND PARTICLEBOARD

Two additional manufactured materials are commonly used in woodworking:

■ Fiber-based sheet materials, or *fiberboards,* are made from wood that has been reduced to cellulose fibers, then reconstituted.

■ Particle-based materials, or *particleboards,* are made from small pieces of wood of various sizes that have been glued back together.

Generally, both of these products are weaker than plywood, and they do not hold fasteners as well. (*SEE FIGURE 5-10.*) Some of them are not as stable. But they are less expensive and offer other useful characteristics.

5-10 This simple experiment shows the relative stiffness of solid wood, plywood, and particleboard. All three boards are precisely the same size and are loaded with the same amount of weight. The wooden board (*top*) sags the least, followed by the plywood (*middle*). The particleboard (*bottom*) is the weakest of the three materials.

FIBERBOARD

When making fiberboard, the manufacturer breaks down the wood by chopping, grinding, and heating until it separates into individual fibers. These fibers are then bonded back together in a process known as *interfelting*. There are many different ways to interfelt wood fibers, but the most common is to compress and heat them at the same time. This turns the lignin on the outside of the cellulose fibers semi-liquid and sticks them to one another. Occasionally, resins, glues, or other binding agents are added to improve the bond. Manufacturers may add other chemicals such as alum, asphalt, wax, preservatives, and fire retarders to improve the strength, durability, water resistance, and fire resistance of the finished material.

There are four types of fiberboard:

■ *Insulation board* is a lightweight material (less than 31 pounds per cubic foot (pcf). It's used mostly in construction for products such as sheathing and ceiling tiles.

■ *Hardboard* is much heavier, anywhere from 31 to 90 pcf. This is what you get when you ask for Masonite at a lumberyard. There are two types of hardboard — *tempered* and *standard*. Tempered hardboard is sprayed with resins *after* it's hot-pressed, then baked. This makes the material hard, strong, water resistant, and somewhat brittle. Standard hardboard is not treated and is softer and more bendable. Hardboard is also used to make siding, paneling, and pegboard. (*See Figure 5-11.*)

■ *Medium-density fiberboard,* or MDF, is made by adding resin before it's hot-pressed. This produces a medium-weight material (between 31 and 55 pcf) that's very stable and remains perfectly flat. Additionally, it has an extremely smooth surface and can be routed and molded like solid wood. (*See Figure 5-12.*)

■ *Laminated paperboard* is made in two steps. First, the wood fibers are made into paper, then layers of paper are pressed together. Often, the outside layers are printed with a color or wood-grain pattern. Paperboard is commonly used to make nonstructural cabinet parts, signs, and displays.

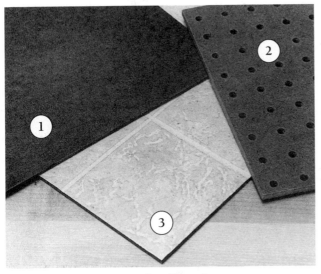

5-11 Woodworkers use hardboard in several different forms. *Tempered hardboard* (1) makes good patterns, templates, drawer bottoms, and cabinet backs. It also makes a durable workbench surface. *Pegboard* (2) is used in millions of homes and small workshops to organize tools and other items. And many *decorative panels* (3) are hardboard sheets that have been textured and printed with colors and patterns.

5-12 Medium-density fiberboard, or MDF, is designed to be easily machined. It can be sawed, drilled, shaped, molded, and routed just like solid wood. Because it has a fine texture, the cut surfaces are extremely smooth. It also takes paint well.

PARTICLEBOARD

Particleboard is made from wood particles of all descriptions, from superfine sawdust to large strands and wafers. After being chipped, planed, or ground up, these particles are dried, sprayed with adhesive resin, and pressed into panels.

The specific properties of a panel are determined by the adhesive used, the density of the sheet, and the size and shape of the particles. Consequently, particleboard is graded with a three-character code that indicates these variables. The first character tells you the adhesive type; the second, the density; and the third, the particle size.

ADHESIVE

1 tells you that the particles are bonded together with a glue intended for interior uses only.

2 indicates that the glue will endure both the weather outdoors and wet locations.

DENSITY

H denotes high density. This material weighs over 53 pounds per cubic foot.

M indicates medium density. The material weighs between 38 and 53 pounds per cubic foot.

L means low density, less than 38 pounds per cubic foot.

PARTICLE SIZE

1 indicates that the material is made from extremely small particles — fiber bundles — that are only slightly larger than individual wood fibers. The surface tends to be very smooth.

2 is for run-of-the-mill sawdust-size particles. The surface is flat but not smooth to the touch.

3 indicates large particles such as planer shavings. These produce a fairly rough surface.

F stands for flakes, wood bits that are somewhat larger than sawdust or shavings. The resulting surface is very rough but fairly even.

W tells you that the material is made from large strands or wafers, and the surface is likely rough and uneven.

As the particles get larger, the panels become stronger and stiffer. (*SEE FIGURE 5-13.*) Particleboard made from F- and W-size particles are strong enough to be used for structural panels in construction. Manufacturers also increase the strength by aligning the wood grain in the particles. *Oriented strand board* is made from W-size particles laid down in layers. The wood grain in each layer is at right angles to the adjacent layers, similar to plywood. Although it's still weaker than plywood, oriented strand material is a good deal stronger than ordinary particleboard.

Most of the particleboard used in furniture making and cabinetmaking is made with interior glue and has a medium density. The particle size determines how the material will be used. Craftsmen generally make case parts from 1-M-1 and 1-M-2 particleboard, and countertops from 1-M-2 and 1-M-3. Shelving can be made from 1-M-1, 1-M-2, or 1-M-3. There are also panels made with special *resin-based coatings* (such as Melamine) that are manufactured especially for making cabinets, shelves, and built-ins. (*SEE FIGURE 5-14.*)

5-13 The most common type of particleboard is made from sawdust-size bits of wood (1). This is used in making furniture and cabinets. Materials made from larger particles are more often used for construction. For example, cedar closet lining (2) is made from aromatic red cedar *flakes,* about the size of planer shavings. Roof sheathing and floor underlayment (3) is made from chip-size pieces of wood or *wafers.* This is much rougher than particleboard made from sawdust, but it's also much stronger.

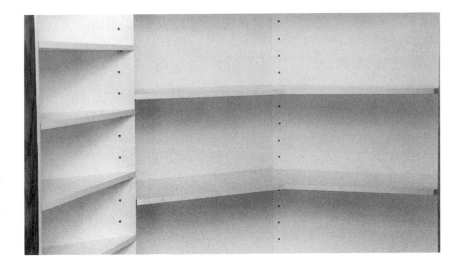

5-14 The particleboard used to make the shelving in this storage closet is coated on both sides with a layer of plastic resin, about $\frac{1}{100}$ inch thick. Although extremely thin, this plastic produces a smooth, hard finish. It's also waterproof and chemical resistant.

THE FOREST PRODUCTS LABORATORY: ANSWERS TO YOUR QUESTIONS

From humble beginnings in 1910, the Forest Products Laboratory (FPL) has grown to become the largest and most comprehensive research facility ever built to study wood and wood materials. An arm of the U.S. Department of Agriculture, the FPL occupies 13 buildings on 22 acres at the University of Wisconsin in Madison. It brings together over 200 specialists in tree botany, forest management, lumbering, sawyering, plywood, composites, adhesives, fasteners, wood engineering — every facet of the wood industry.

The focus of FPL research is threefold:

■ Developing new products and techniques to make better use of wood

■ Making wood products and buildings safer

■ Sustaining the forests and their ecosystems

The Forest Products Laboratory conducts research on every conceivable way in which wood can be used. This miniature paper plant, for example, is a test bed for new products that can be made from wood fibers. Although the products and the processes developed by the FPL are patented, they are licensed free of charge to American manufacturers.

(continued) ▷

THE FOREST PRODUCTS LABORATORY: ANSWERS TO YOUR QUESTIONS — CONTINUED

But research is only half their mission. The other half is *information*. The FPL answers tens of thousands of questions every year on wood and woodworking materials. The scientists I've talked to in Madison tell me they occupy half their time on the phone, sharing what they've learned. Furthermore, they have published hundreds of technical reports, scientific articles, and handbooks on specific wood topics. The FPL has organized these reports into several general areas. Those areas that are of particular interest to woodworkers are:

■ Sawing Wood and Related Processes — sawing, cutting, slicing, hardwood and softwood grades, specifications, and standards

■ Drying Wood — drying rates, shrinking and swelling, moisture content, stresses, methods including air drying, kiln drying, and solar drying

■ Fiber and Particle Products, Plywood, and Veneer — wood and nonwood composite materials, plywood, fiberboard, and particleboard

■ Wood Bonding Systems — adhesive types and characteristics, gluing wood and other materials, durability of adhesives, wood laminating

■ Furniture Manufacture and Woodworking — properties of wood, glues and gluing, wood preservation, drying and seasoning, sawing, and finishing

If you ask, the FPL will send you a list of the publications in each of these areas and help you locate specific publications that may be of interest to you. Write:

Information
Forest Products Laboratory
One Gifford Pinchot Drive
Madison, WI 53705

If you have computer access to the Internet, the address of the FPL's home page is:

http://www.fs.fed.us/outernet/fpl/welcome.html

Have you ever cut a board a little short and wished you had a "wood stretcher?" Well, here it is. This special press at the Forest Products Laboratory is capable of generating a million pounds of tension or compression, letting you stretch or squeeze boards, lumber, and even giant timbers. Researchers use the monster press to determine the strengths of wood products and methods of construction.

In addition to conducting labora-tory tests on wood and wood products, the Forest Products Laboratory does practical studies on all kinds of construction methods and materials. This wooden bridge at the entrance to one of the FPL's many buildings was built with dozens of different fasteners to glean a better understanding of how each fastener type performs in use.

PROJECTS

6

CONTEMPORARY KEEPING CHEST

For hundreds of years, small "keeping" chests have been used to store jewelry, silverware, documents, and other small items. This particular chest is patterned after a traditional mule chest, with a single drawer in the bottom. A lift-out tray helps make the top compartment more accessible (A).

While the construction is traditional, the styling is contemporary. The joinery is used as a decorative element — the corner splines mix several wood species to create a geometric pattern at the corners. This pattern is repeated on the top by slicing splines and inlaying the slices (B). To prevent all this

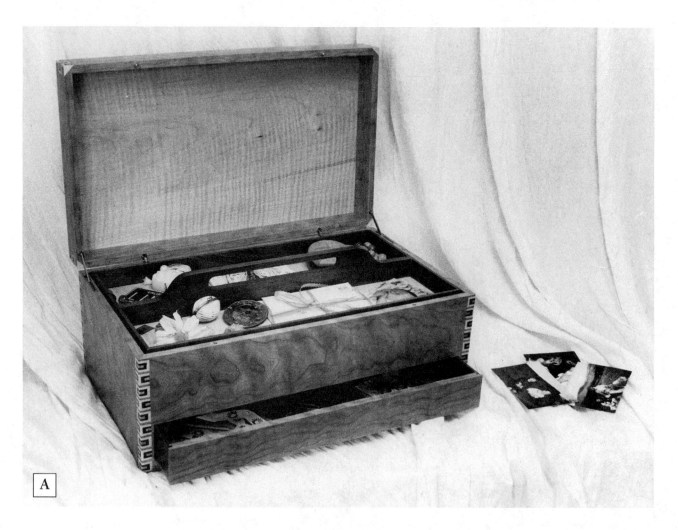

A

geometry from appearing too busy, the lines of the piece were kept simple. The surfaces are perfectly straight and flat, and the hardware has been carefully concealed (*C and D*).

When using contrasting woods in a project like this, you must think ahead. Wood colors change when you apply a finish. Furthermore, most woods darken with age; a few, such as walnut and mahogany, grow lighter. If you mix cherry and walnut, the joint between them will be highly visible for a time, but as the cherry darkens and the walnut lightens, it will become less so. Before you cut good wood, glue up different combinations of woods, apply a finish, and let them sit for several weeks to help decide which combinations will look best.

Also remember that different woods expand and contract at different rates. This will stress the joints and may distort the wood if you glue large surfaces together. To minimize this problem on the keeping chest, we kept the splines and the inlays small — there are no large glued surfaces. Where we joined large pieces of contrasting woods (such as the top and sides), we used floating joints to let the woods expand and contract independently.

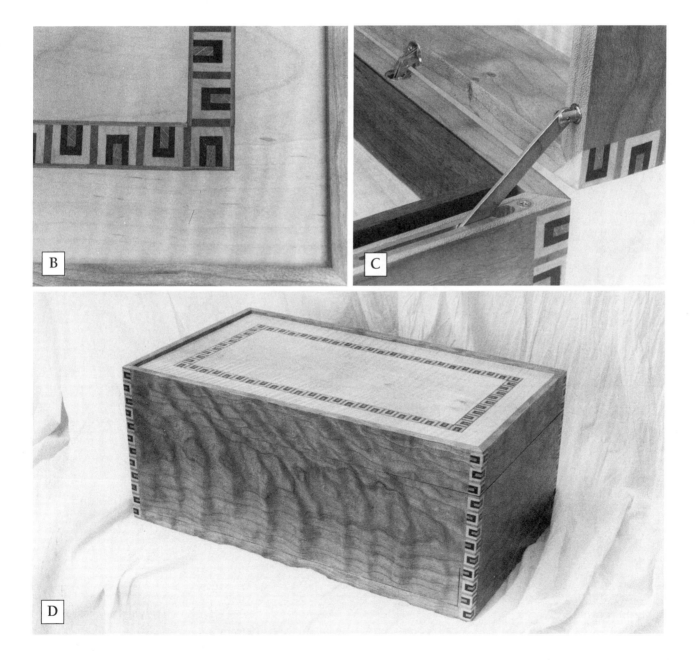

B

C

D

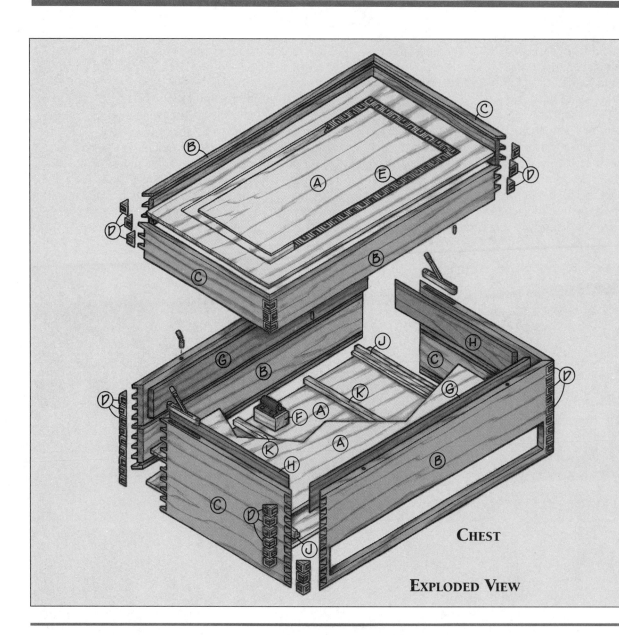

CHEST

EXPLODED VIEW

MATERIALS LIST (FINISHED DIMENSIONS)
Parts
Chest

A. Top/bottom/
    divider (3)   1/4″ x 11⅜″ x 20½″

B. Front/
    back (2)   ½″ x 9¼″* x 21″

C. Sides (2)   ½″ x 9¼″* x 12″

D. Splines (48)†   7/16″ x ⅝″ x ⅞″

E. Inlay (total)†   ⅛″ x ¾″ x 52″

F. Latch mount   1″ x 1⅛″ x 2″

G. Front/back tray
    supports (2)   1/4″ x 2⅜″ x 20″

H. Side tray
    supports (2)   1/4″ x 2⅜″ x 11″

J. Drawer
    guides (2)   ½″ x ½″ x 11″

K. Drawer
    runners (2)   ⅜″ x ½″ x 11″

Tray

L. Tray front/
    back (2)   1/4″ x 1½″ x 19¹⁵/₁₆″

M. Tray
    sides (2)   1/4″ x 1½″ x 10¹⁵/₁₆″

N. Tray
    divider   ½″ x 2¾″ x 19¹¹/₁₆″

P. Tray bottoms
    (2)   1/4″ x 5⁵/₃₂″ x 19¹¹/₁₆″

*This dimension will be reduced to 9⅛″ when you cut the lid from the box.
†These parts are glued up from several different wood species. Refer to Step 1, page 80.

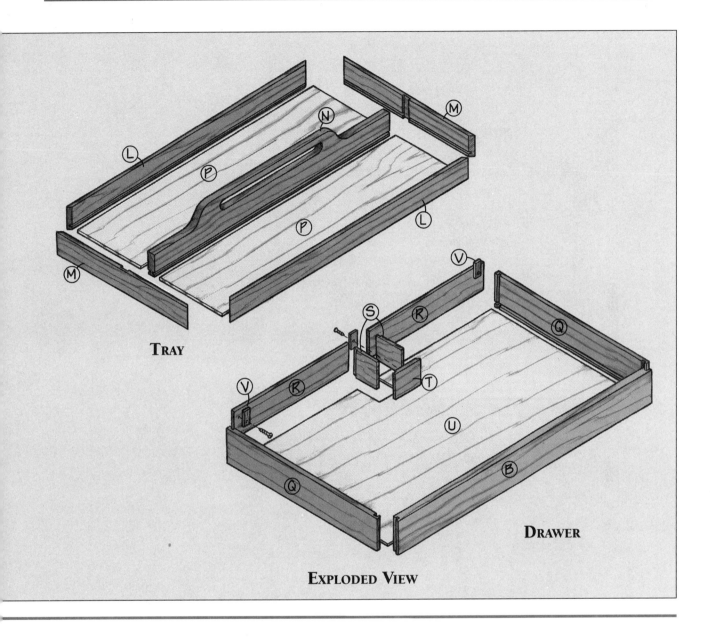

TRAY

EXPLODED VIEW

DRAWER

Drawer

Q. Drawer
   sides (2) ¼" x 2⅛" x 11⅛"
R. Drawer
   backs (2) ¼" x 1⅝" x 8⅞"
S. Drawer notch
   sides (2) ¼" x 1⅝" x 2"
T. Drawer notch
   back ¼" x 1⅝" x 1½"

U. Drawer
   bottom ¼" x 10¾" x 19¼"
V. Kickers (2) ⅜" x ½" x 1"

Hardware

⁷⁄₁₆" (10mm) Barrel hinges (2)
2¾" Jewelry box lid supports (2)
Tutch latch and mounting screws
#4 x ⅝" Brass flathead wood
   screws (17)
⅛" dia. x ¾" Brass pins (2)

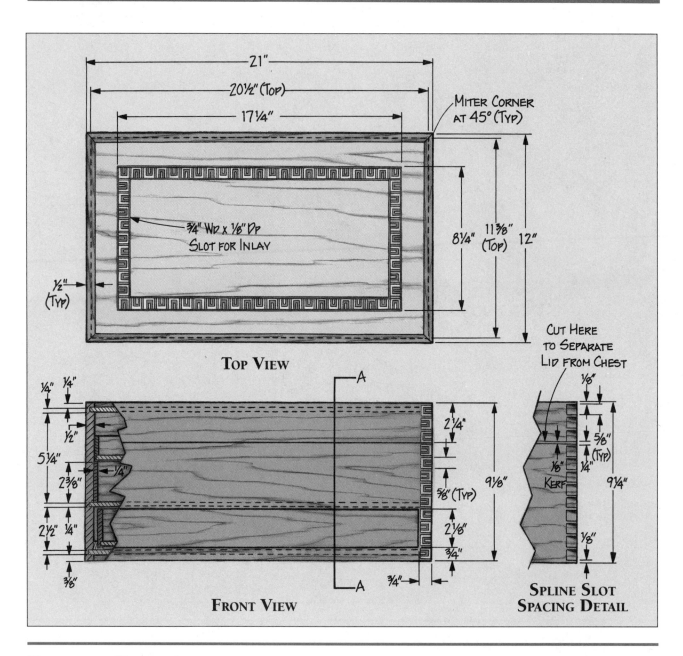

PLAN OF PROCEDURE

1 Select the stock and cut the parts. To make this project, you need approximately 12 board feet of 4/4 (four-quarters) lumber. You can use any cabinet-grade wood, and you can mix wood species, as we have done here. The chest shown is made from five different hardwoods, two of which have curly grain:

- Cherry (curly) — front, back, sides
- Maple (curly) — top, bottom, divider, tray bottoms, drawer bottom, latch mount, drawer guides, drawer runners
- Walnut — tray supports, tray front, tray back,

tray sides, tray divider, drawer sides, drawer backs, drawer notch sides, drawer notch back, inlay, splines

- White ash — inlay, splines
- Red oak — inlay, splines

Carefully plan which boards you'll use to make specific parts. On a band saw, resaw the boards selected for the ¼-inch-thick parts, cutting them in half. Plane the boards to thickness, then cut the front, back, sides, top, bottom, and divider to size. Miter the ends of the front, back, and sides at 45 degrees, as shown on the *Top View*. Do *not* make the other parts yet.

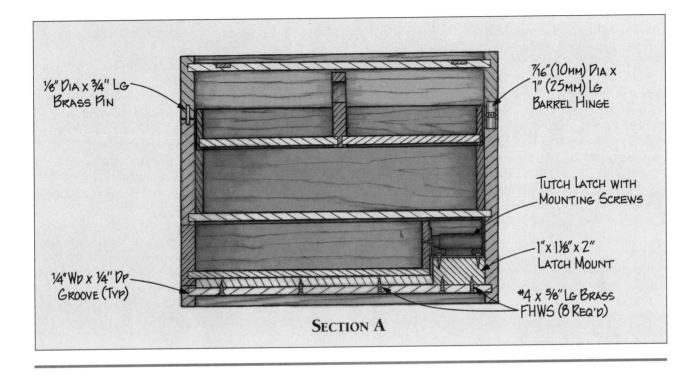

1/8" DIA X 3/4" LG
BRASS PIN

7/16"(10MM) DIA X
1" (25MM) LG
BARREL HINGE

TUTCH LATCH WITH
MOUNTING SCREWS

1" X 1⅛" X 2"
LATCH MOUNT

1/4" WD X 1/4" DP
GROOVE (TYP)

#4 X 5/8" LG BRASS
FHWS (8 REQ'D)

SECTION A

2 **Make the drawer front.** Cut the drawer front from the chest front so the wood grain will appear to be continuous when the drawer is closed. To do this, lay out the drawer front as shown in the *Front View*. Drill 1/16-inch-diameter holes at each corner. Insert a #4 (or smaller) fret blade through one of the holes and cut out the drawer front with a scroll saw or coping saw. Don't cut through to the edge or end of the board. When you've finished cutting, there should be a rectangular hole in the front. The fine blade will leave a smooth surface, so you should only have to do a little touch-up sanding on the sawed surfaces.

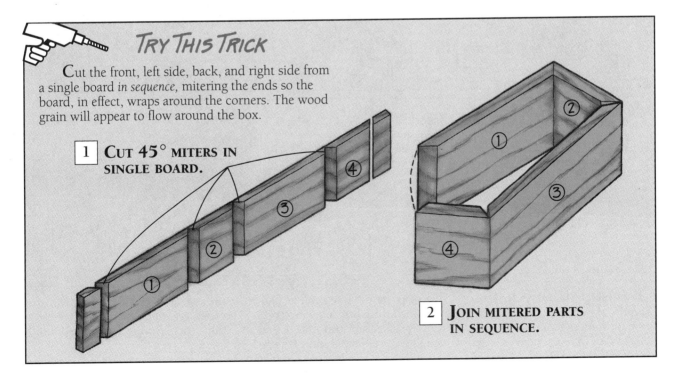

Try This Trick

Cut the front, left side, back, and right side from a single board *in sequence*, mitering the ends so the board, in effect, wraps around the corners. The wood grain will appear to flow around the box.

1 **Cut 45° miters in single board.**

2 **Join mitered parts in sequence.**

3 Make the splines and inlays. The miter joints at the corners of the chest are reinforced with decorative splines. The pattern that these splines create is repeated in the inlays at the top. Although this pattern appears complex, it's simple to make.

To create the splines, cut four strips of white ash (or another light-colored wood) ⁷⁄₁₆ inch thick, ⅝ inch wide, and about 16 inches long. As shown in the *Spline Strip Detail,* rout a ⅜-inch-wide, ¹¹⁄₃₂-inch-deep groove down the middle of each strip, cut pieces of walnut (or another dark-colored wood) to fill these grooves, and glue them in place. Let the glue dry, then rout a ⅛-inch-wide, ¼-inch-deep groove in each strip. Cut pieces of red oak (or another medium-colored wood) to fill the grooves and glue them in place. When the glue dries, cut the spline stock into 1-inch lengths. This will give you about 8 extra splines for test pieces.

To make the inlays, start with two strips of ash, ⅝ inch square and 16 inches long. As shown in the *Inlay Strip Detail,* cut grooves in the strips and fill them with different colors of woods — just as you did when making the spline strips. Cut ⅛-inch-thick, ⅝-inch-wide, 16-inch-long pieces of cherry (or what-

ever wood you used to make the front, back, and sides), and glue a piece to each of the inlay strips.

Cut the inlay strips in 1-inch lengths and glue 28 pieces edge to edge. Note that every other piece is reversed 180 degrees, so the grooves face one way, then the other. Let the glue dry, sand the surfaces flush, and sandwich the assembly between four strips of cherry veneer — two on the top, two on the bottom. When the glue dries, the inlay assembly should be ¾ inch thick. On a band saw, resaw the assembly into ⁵⁄₃₂-inch-thick strips. (*SEE FIGURE 6-1.*)

4 Install the inlays. Using a coping saw and a chisel, cut the inlays so the ends meet, as shown on the *Inlay Corner Joint Detail.* Temporarily tape the inlay strips together to form a rectangle and measure the dimensions of the rectangle — they will probably differ slightly from what is shown on the drawings. Lay out the inlay on the chest top, using the new dimensions.

Rout ¾-inch-wide, ⅛-inch-deep grooves for the inlay in the top, then glue the inlay strips in the grooves. They should be just a little proud of the surface. When the glue dries, scrape and sand them flush.

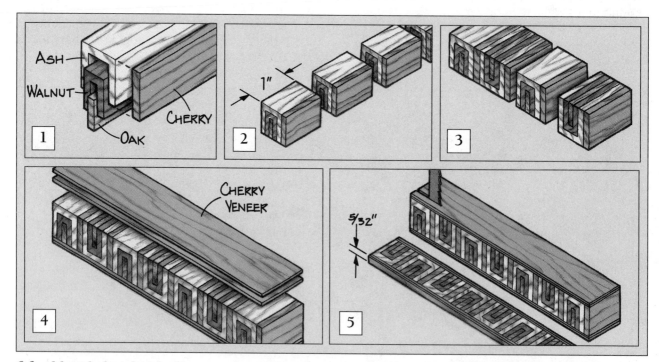

6-1 Although the inlays look complex, they're made with a series of simple cuts and assemblies. (1) Cut four different wood species into strips, rout grooves so three of the strips nest in one another, and glue the fourth beside the nest. (2) Cut the glued-up strips into 1-inch lengths. (3) Glue the short lengths together edge to edge. (4) Sandwich the assembly between sheets of veneer. (5) Slice the assembly into thin strips, cutting across the grain.

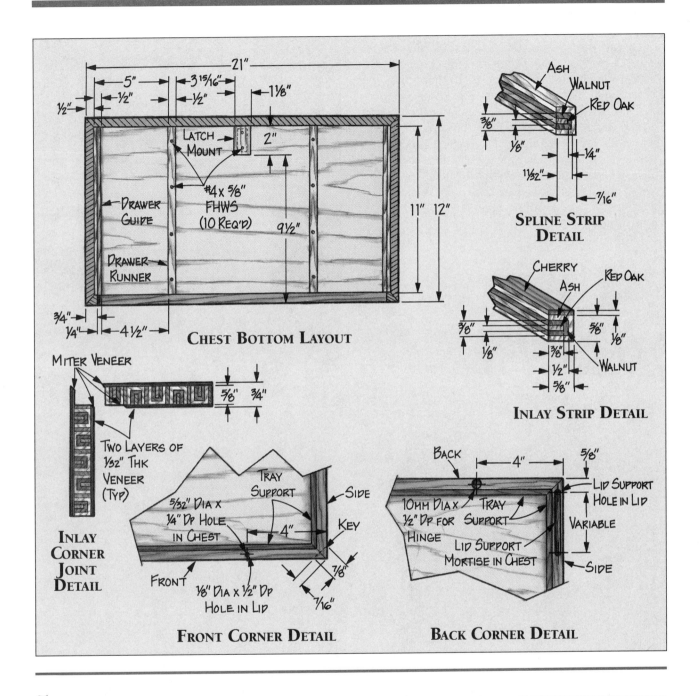

CHEST BOTTOM LAYOUT

SPLINE STRIP DETAIL

INLAY STRIP DETAIL

INLAY CORNER JOINT DETAIL

FRONT CORNER DETAIL

BACK CORNER DETAIL

5 **Cut the grooves in the chest parts.** The top, bottom, and divider all float in ¼-inch-wide, ¼-inch-deep grooves in the front, back, and sides, as shown in *Section A*. Make these grooves with a dado cutter or router.

6 **Assemble the chest.** Finish sand the top, bottom, divider, front, back, and sides. Assemble the parts, gluing the mitered corners together. Do *not* glue the top, bottom, or divider in their grooves. Let them float so they can move freely.

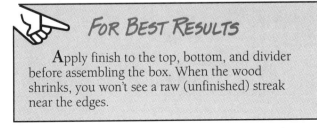

FOR BEST RESULTS

Apply finish to the top, bottom, and divider before assembling the box. When the wood shrinks, you won't see a raw (unfinished) streak near the edges.

7 **Install the splines.** The splines rest in ⅝-inch-wide, ⁷⁄₁₆-inch-deep slots cut across the corners at a 45-degree angle to the surfaces, as shown on the *Front Corner Detail.* To make these slots, make a jig to hold the chest at the proper angle to the cutter, as shown in *FIGURE 6-2.* Cut or rout the slots in the corners, spacing them as shown in the *Spline Slot Spacing Detail.*

Glue the splines in the slots, reversing every other spline 180 degrees, as shown in the *Front View.* (The pattern should be the same as the inlay.) When the glue dries, cut and sand the spline flush with the chest surfaces. *(SEE FIGURE 6-3.)*

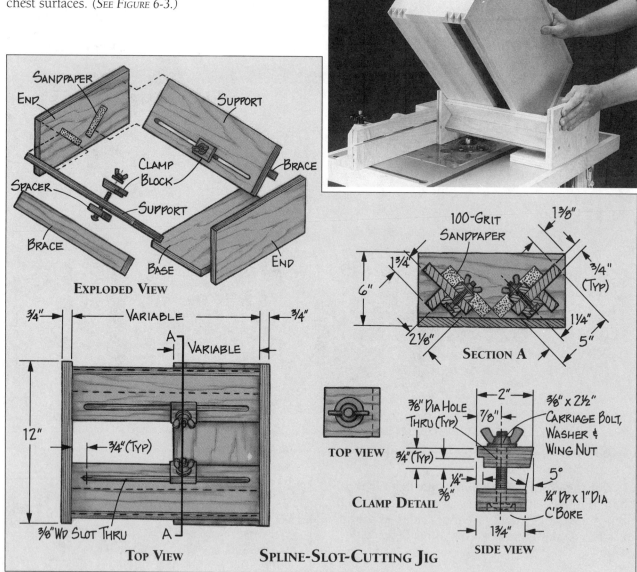

EXPLODED VIEW

TOP VIEW

SPLINE-SLOT-CUTTING JIG

SECTION A

TOP VIEW

CLAMP DETAIL

SIDE VIEW

6-2 Use a dado cutter or a table- mounted router (shown) with the *Spline-Slot-Cutting Jig* to make the spline slots. Rest the chest in the jig, making sure the clamp blocks hold it tight against the jig's side. Position the router table fence to make the first set of slots and cut a slot in each corner, rotating the chest as you work. Reposition the fence for the next set, and repeat. Continue until you have made 12 slots in each corner.

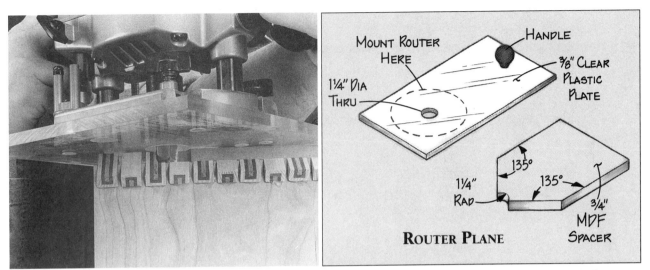

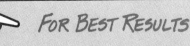

6-3 After gluing the splines in the slots, trim them flush with the chest surfaces. One of the easiest ways to do this is to use a router plane. Replace the router base with a plastic plate and a spacer, as shown. Mount a straight bit in the router and adjust the depth of cut so the tip of the bit is even with the bottom surface of the spacer. Rest the spacer on the chest, turn on the router, and cut away the protruding parts of the splines.

8 Cut the lid from the chest. Cut the lid from the chest on a table saw, using a blade that cuts a ⅛-inch-wide kerf. Position the fence so the blade cuts just under the third spline from the top, as shown in the *Spline Slot Spacing Detail.* Cut the front, then the two sides. Before cutting the back, insert ⅛-inch-thick spacers in the cuts you have already made and clamp the lid to the box. The spacers and clamps will hold the lid steady as you make the last cut.

9 Cut the tray and drawer parts. Measure the assembled chest — the dimensions may have changed slightly from what is shown in the drawings. Cut the tray and drawer parts to size, adjusting the dimensions as needed. Also cut the tray supports, latch mount, guides, and runners. Miter the ends of the tray front, back, and sides, as shown in the *Tray/Top View,* and the ends of the tray supports, as shown in the *Front Corner Detail* and *Back Corner Detail.*

10 Cut the tray joinery. The parts of the tray are joined with miters, dadoes, and grooves. Cut ¼-inch-wide, ⅛-inch-deep grooves near the bottom edges of the tray front, back, sides, and dividers to hold the tray bottoms, as shown in *Section B.* Also make ½-inch-wide, ⅛-inch-deep dadoes in the tray sides to hold the tray divider.

11 Cut the tray divider profile. Lay out the profile of the handhold on the tray divider, as shown in the *Tray/Front View.* Drill ¾-inch-diameter holes to mark the ends of the handhold, then cut away the waste between the holes with a scroll saw or a coping saw. Cut the outside shape (top edge) of the handhold and sand the sawed edges.

12 Assemble and fit the tray. Finish sand the parts of the tray and the tray supports. Glue the tray front, back, sides, and divider together. As you assemble these parts, slip the tray bottoms into their grooves, but *don't* glue them in place; let them float.

Place the tray supports inside the chest. Don't bother gluing them in place; they will stay where you want them without glue. (This also lets you remove them easily should you want to add dividers or another tray sometime in the future.) Rest the tray on top of the supports. If it seems snug, sand or scrape the outside surfaces until it lifts easily in and out of the chest.

For Best Results

Apply finish to the tray bottoms before assembling the tray. This prevents raw wood from showing when the bottoms shrink.

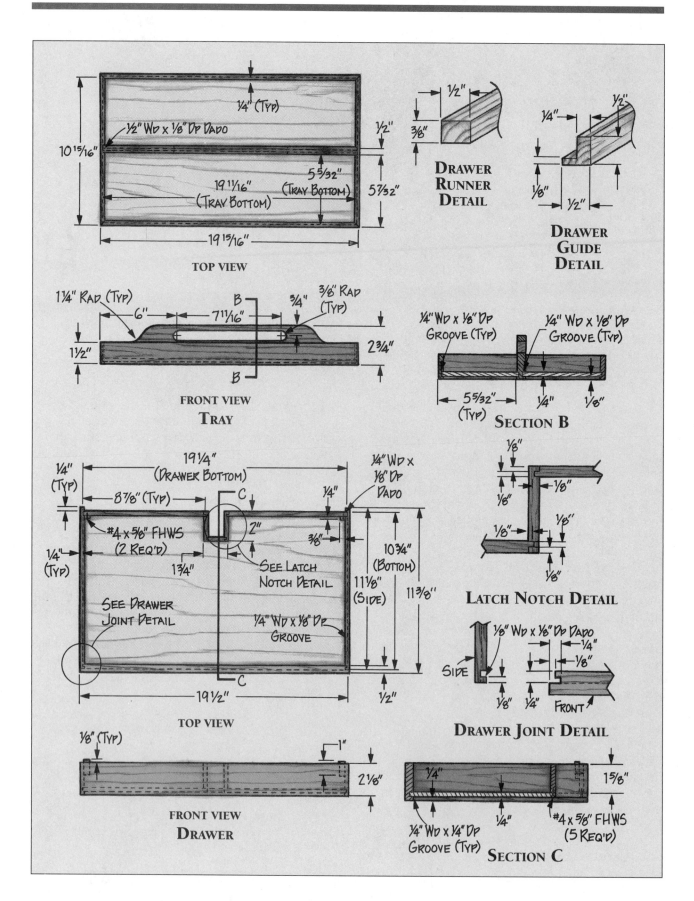

¼" (Typ)

½" Wd x ⅛" Dp Dado

10¹⁵⁄₁₆"

½"

5⁵⁄₃₂"
(Tray Bottom)

19¹¹⁄₁₆"
(Tray Bottom)

5⁷⁄₃₂"

19¹⁵⁄₁₆"

TOP VIEW

½"

3⁄8"

DRAWER RUNNER DETAIL

¼"

½"

⅛"

½"

DRAWER GUIDE DETAIL

1¼" Rad (Typ)

6"

7¹¹⁄₁₆"

3⁄4"

3⁄8" Rad (Typ)

B

B

1½"

2¾"

FRONT VIEW
TRAY

¼" Wd x ⅛" Dp Groove (Typ)

¼" Wd x ⅛" Dp Groove (Typ)

5⁵⁄₃₂"
(Typ)

¼"

⅛"

SECTION B

19¼"
(Drawer Bottom)

¼" (Typ)

8⅞" (Typ)

¼" Wd x ⅛" Dp Dado

¼"

#4 x ⅝" FHWS
(2 Req'd)

2"

3⁄8"

See Latch Notch Detail

¼" (Typ)

1¾"

See Drawer Joint Detail

¼" Wd x ⅛" Dp Groove

10¾"
(Bottom)

11⅛"
(Side)

11⅜"

19½"

½"

TOP VIEW

⅛"

⅛"

⅛"

⅛"

⅛"

⅛"

LATCH NOTCH DETAIL

⅛" Wd x ⅛" Dp Dado

¼"

⅛"

SIDE

⅛"

¼"

FRONT

DRAWER JOINT DETAIL

⅛" (Typ)

1"

2⅛"

FRONT VIEW
DRAWER

¼"

1⅝"

¼" Wd x ¼" Dp
Groove (Typ)

¼"

#4 x ⅝" FHWS
(5 Req'd)

SECTION C

13 Cut the drawer joinery. The drawer bottom floats in grooves, while the other parts are joined with tongue-and-dado joints. Cut a ¼-inch-wide, ¼-inch-deep groove in the drawer front and ¼-inch-wide, ⅛-inch-deep grooves in the drawer sides to hold the bottom, as shown in the *Drawer/Top View* and *Section C.*

To make the front corner joints, cut ⅛-inch-wide, ¼-inch-deep grooves in the ends of the drawer front, as shown in the *Drawer Joint Detail.* Cut the *interior* side of these grooves short, making tongues just ⅛ inch long. Then cut ⅛-inch-wide, ⅛-inch-deep dadoes in the sides to fit these tongues. For the back corner joints, cut ¼-inch-wide, ⅛-inch-deep dadoes in the sides to hold the backs.

To join the backs, notch sides, and notch back, cut ⅛-inch-wide, ⅛-inch-deep rabbets in the inside ends of the drawer backs and both ends of the notch back, as shown in the *Latch Notch Detail.* This will create small tongues on the ends of these parts. Cut ⅛-inch-wide, ⅛-inch-deep dadoes in the notch sides to fit these tongues. Drill 1/16-inch-diameter pilot holes through the back for the screws that hold the kickers.

Finally, cut ¼-inch-wide, ⅜-inch-deep rabbets in the drawer guides, as shown in the *Drawer Guide Detail,* making them L-shaped.

14 Assemble the drawer. Finish sand the drawer parts, then glue together the front, sides, backs, notch sides, and notch back. Before the glue dries, slip the drawer bottom into its groove to square the drawer assembly. After the glue dries, align the back edge of the drawer bottom flush with the drawer backs and mark the outline of the latch notch. Remove the bottom and cut the notch in it with a scroll saw or band saw. Replace the drawer bottom and attach it to the drawer backs and notch back with flathead wood screws.

FOR BEST RESULTS

Apply finish to the drawer bottom before assembling the drawer. Also, glue up the drawer parts upside down on a flat surface — this ensures that the assembled drawer will be flat.

15 Fit the drawer in the chest. Carefully measure the distance from the back of the drawer opening to the front of the chest — it may have changed slightly from the 11½ inches shown on the *Chest Bottom Layout.* Attach the magnetic plate from the

Tutch latch to the back surface of the notch back. On a flat surface arrange the drawer, guides, runners, latch mount, and Tutch latch as they will be positioned inside the chest. (Make sure the latch is *closed.*) Slide the latch mount forward and back until the distance from the back of the mount to the drawer front is precisely the same as that between the drawer opening back and the chest front. Mark the position of the latch on the mount, then secure it with screws.

Attach the latch mount and the drawer runners to the chest bottom with flathead wood screws, driving the screws up through the bottom. (Do *not* glue the mount or the runners to the bottom; the glue will restrict the wood movement, while the screws bend slightly as the wood moves.) Rest the drawer guides in places against the chest sides, then slide the drawer into the opening. **Note:** It's not necessary to attach the guides permanently; the drawer will hold them in place. If you do want to secure them, glue them to the sides but *not* the bottom.

Test the action of the drawer. You must be able to push the drawer in far enough to release the Tutch latch. The latch will push the drawer out about ½ inch — just far enough for you to get a good grip on the front edge and slide it the rest of the way out of the chest. When you slide the drawer back into the chest, push it in far enough to close the latch. When the latch is closed it should hold the drawer front flush with the chest front. If the drawer binds when it slides in and out, sand or scrape the surfaces that rub until it works smoothly.

TRY THIS TRICK

Install the screws that hold the latch mount in countersunk *slots,* about ¼ inch long. This will let you adjust the position of the latch slightly so it holds the drawer precisely flush with the chest front.

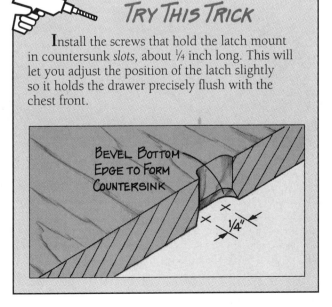

BEVEL BOTTOM EDGE TO FORM COUNTERSINK

¼"

16 **Hinge the lid to the chest.** Place the lid on the chest and mark the positions of the hinges on the back, as shown in the *Back Corner Detail*. Draw lines across the seam so both the lid and the box are marked identically. Using a small square, transfer these lines to the back edges of the chest and lid. At each mark, drill a 7/16-inch-diameter (or 10-millimeter-diameter), 1/2-inch-deep hole for the barrel of a hinge.

Carefully measure the lid supports you have purchased to determine the sizes of the holes and mortises you need to make to install them. Lay out the positions of the lid supports on the edges of the sides. Drill holes in the bottom edges of the lids to attach the support arms. Then rout mortises in the top edges of the chest to hold the support housings. (*SEE FIGURE 6-4.*)

Temporarily install the hinges and the lid supports and test the action of the lid. Also check that the lid sits squarely on the chest, flush with the front, back, and sides. If not, you may have to cut plugs for the holes and the mortises and reinstall the hardware.

When you're satisfied the lid is properly hinged to the chest, mark the holes for the alignment pins, as shown on the *Front Corner Detail*. Remove the hinges and the lid supports, then drill 1/8-inch-diameter, 1/2-inch-deep holes in the lid and 5/32-inch-diameter, 1/4-inch-deep holes in the chest. These holes will hold pins that will help align the lid when it's closed.

17 **Finish the chest.** Remove the drawer, tray, latch mount, and any loose wooden parts such as the tray supports and the drawer guides. Detach the latch from its mount and set the hardware aside. Do any necessary touch-up sanding, then apply a finish to all unfinished wood surfaces. Let it dry thoroughly, rub it out, and reassemble the chest. Attach the hinges, lid supports, and brass pins permanently with epoxy cement.

Finally, attach the kickers to the back of the drawer with flathead wood screws. These small blocks serve two purposes. They prevent the drawer from tilting forward as it slides forward, and they keep it from being pulled completely out of the chest.

WHERE TO FIND IT

Barrel hinges, mortised lid supports, and 10mm drill bits are available from:

The Woodworker's Store
21801 Industrial Boulevard
Rogers, MN 55374

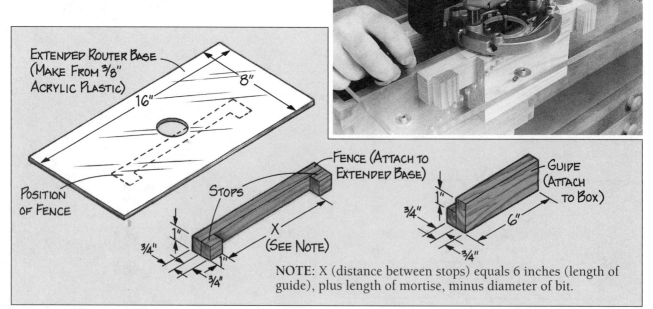

6-4 To rout the mortises for the lid supports, you must balance your router on the top edges of the chest and make a perfectly straight cut, stopping when the mortise is just the right length. To help do this, first attach your router to an extended router base — a large piece of plastic or plywood. Make a fence with stops and attach it to the bottom surface of the extended base with double-faced carpet tape. Also make a guide and attach it to the box with tape. The extended base will help you balance the router. The fence and the guide will keep the router moving in a straight line, and the stops will halt the cut automatically.

7

HERRINGBONE CUTTING BOARD

One of the most distressing dilemmas a woodworker faces is what to do with scraps. Few of us can bring ourselves to throw away any piece of wood (larger than a toothpick) that we've paid good money for. Consequently, most of us are on the lookout for good "scrap wood" projects, and this is one of them. This cutting board is assembled from small strips of left-over stock. By cleverly arranging the pieces, you can create attractive geometric designs such as this herringbone pattern (A).

A cutting board is a simple project, but it requires some careful thought. When gluing up stock, you must carefully arrange the wood grain so the assembled parts all expand and contract together, without stressing the glue joints. Ideally, the wood grain should all run in the same direction.

The parts in a herringbone pattern are mitered on the adjoining ends. If you assemble the parts with the flat grain showing on the face of the cutting board, the wood grain in half the parts will be perpendicular to the other half. The seams will open up as the wood moves, as large miter joints always do. To avoid this, the parts in this project are oriented so the *end grain* shows on the face (B). All

the wood grain is parallel; the assembly shrinks and swells as if it were a solid board.

Showing the end grain on the face of a cutting board has other advantages. Knives stay sharp longer — the cutting edges bury themselves between the wood fibers rather than slice through them. And the cutting board looks good longer. That's because end grain fibers are split but rarely severed, while flat grain gets chopped up, eventually ruining the surface.

PLAN OF PROCEDURE

1 Select the stock. There is no Materials List for this project; you can make the cutting board as small or as large as you wish. Nor are there any recommended materials; you can use almost any combination of domestic hardwoods. The cutting board shown is made from oak, poplar, maple, cherry, and walnut scraps from ⅛ inch to ¾ inch thick.

Whenever you make a project that will come in contact with the food you eat, give some thought to the potential toxicity of the wood. Never use treated lumber; it's often saturated with chemicals containing arsenic. These may leach out of the wood and taint the food. Also avoid potent "toxic" woods — species that commonly cause allergic reactions, nausea, and other health problems. (See "Toxic Woods" on page 23 for more information.) You may not be sensitive to the chemicals in these woods, but others are.

2 Glue up the scraps. After selecting the wood scraps, cut them to a uniform size, 3 inches wide and 12 inches long. Bevel one edge at 45 degrees. Glue them together with a waterproof glue so the beveled edges are flush with one another. (*SEE FIGURE 7-1.*)

FOR YOUR INFORMATION

As long as you avoid treated and toxic lumber, there is evidence that wood makes a healthier food-preparation surface than other materials, including plastic. Microbiologists at the University of Wisconsin found that three minutes after inoculating wooden cutting boards with *Salmonella, E. coli,* and other bacteria known to cause food poisoning, 99.9 percent of the little critters were dead. In contrast, all the bugs on inoculated plastic boards were still armed and dangerous. Trees generate natural antibiotics to kill bacteria that cause wood rot, and apparently these are also effective against food-poisoning bacteria in small concentrations.

---

3 Cut the assembly into strips. On a table saw, cut the assembly into 1-inch-thick strips, cutting *across* the grain (perpendicular to the length of the glued-up scraps). True each strip by ripping the edges straight. (*SEE FIGURES 7-2 AND 7-3.*)

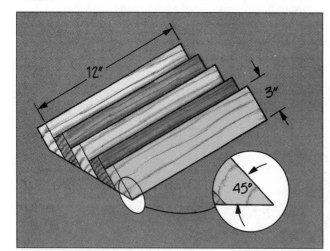

7-1 Bevel the edges of the scraps at 45 degrees, then glue them together face to face so the beveled edges are flush. Epoxy works best for this task — it's waterproof and it doesn't have to cure under pressure to form a strong bond. This is a difficult assembly to clamp together, but if you use epoxy, you don't have to worry about it. Just press the pieces together and let the glue cure.

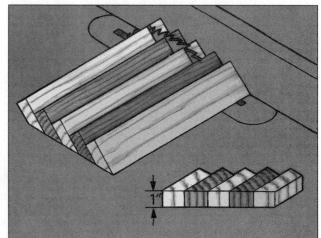

7-2 Using a table saw and a combination blade, cut the glued-up stock into 1-inch-thick strips. *Crosscut* the wood, cutting across the individual boards. Number each strip sequentially as it's cut, always writing the number on the same end. Each piece should appear to be striped, with bars of different colors and grain textures running diagonally across the width.

4 **Glue the strips edge to edge.** Arrange the strips in parallel rows. Turn them so the diagonal stripes alternate directions. For example, arrange the first strip so the stripes run from top left to bottom right. Turn the next strip so they go from bottom left to top right, and so on. This will create a herringbone pattern. After arranging the strips, glue them edge to edge. (*See Figure 7-4.*)

5 **Trim the top and bottom.** Cut across the top and bottom of the assembly to make it rectangular. Discard the scraps — or save them to make an even smaller project. (*See Figure 7-5.*)

6 **Finish the cutting board.** Finish sand the surfaces of the assembled board and apply a nontoxic or low-toxicity finish such as shellac, walnut oil, mineral oil, or water-based lacquer. One of the best finishes for cutting boards is paste wax. It brings out the color of the wood, it's not toxic, it's impervious to water, and it doesn't seal the wood. According to the University of Wisconsin study mentioned on the opposite page, the bacteria-killing properties of wood were less effective when it was *sealed* with a finish.

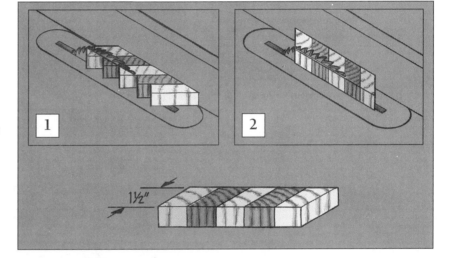

7-3 On each strip, one edge will be fairly straight while the other will have a sawtooth profile. Position the fence about 1⅝ inches away from the blade and trim the sawteeth from all the strips, guiding the straight edges along the fence (1). Then reposition the fence 1½ inches from the blade, turn the strips end for end, and trim the straight edge (2). When you've finished, both edges of the strips should be straight and true.

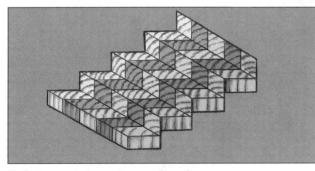

7-4 Arrange the strips so the edges are parallel and the numbered ends all face in the same direction. Turn the even-numbered strips face for face so diagonal stripes of color change direction with every strip. Align the strips so the ends are even and the colors seem to zigzag across the wood. This creates a herringbone pattern. Glue the strips edge to edge with epoxy or another waterproof cement.

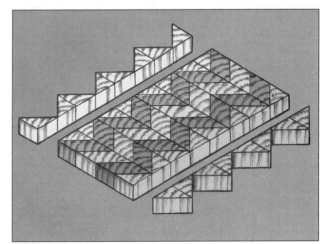

7-5 Once you have glued the strips together, the top and bottom edges of the board will have a saw-tooth profile. Trim the sawteeth with a table saw or a band saw, making the cutting board rectangular.

8

GRANDMOTHER CLOCK

A "grandmother" clock is a small case clock — a pendulum clockworks (or *movement*) in a wooden case, under five feet tall. Except for its size, it has all the attributes of a grandfather (tall case) clock. The movement is enclosed in a *hood* to protect it from dust; the pendulum swings back and forth inside the *waist*, and the entire case rests on a *base* (A).

You face many of the same problems when building a grandmother clock, although its case is typically simpler than that of a grandfather clock. First, you must provide easy access to the face and the pendulum to set the time, wind the clockworks, and set the works in motion. There are two doors on the front of the case — one covering the hood and the other, the waist — for these purposes. Additionally, you have to be able to reach the clockworks for occasional cleaning and maintenance. On this case, the top lifts off and the clock board slides out with the works attached (B).

The moldings on a clock also present a quandary. The wood grain in the moldings at the top of the case and at the waist (dividing the hood from the waist), as well as the base sides, all run perpendicular to the grain in the case sides. Consequently, you cannot glue these pieces in place. They are attached with screws in oversize holes (C). This arrangement allows all the parts to move independently.

A

92

On this particular clock, we decided to make the moldings removable (D). The base and base moldings are glued to the bottom and the bottom spacer, but the entire assembly slides forward, out of the bottom dadoes in the sides. The waist molding is made the same way — it's attached to the middle shelf and middle spacer, and the assembly slides forward out of the shelf dado. The bonnet molding assembly simply lifts off the case. All these assemblies are held in place with screws.

The reason for this unique construction is the way in which the doors are hung. Traditionally, clock doors are hung on semi-concealed knife hinges. These can be a real bear to install, especially when the case is permanently assembled. By making the spacers that hold the hinges removable, you eliminate a lot of grief when it comes time to install the doors.

When building this project, take extra care to protect the movement from sawdust — the delicate gears will not work correctly if they get dirty. Workshops are dusty environments, and it's not uncommon for a woodworker to finish a clock project only to find he has to get the works cleaned before it will run properly.

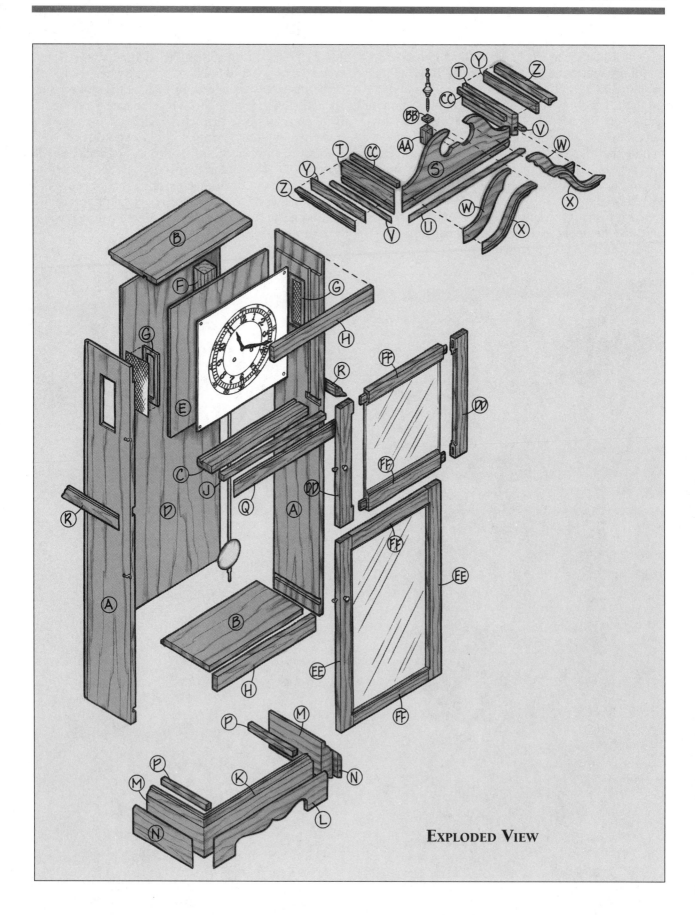

EXPLODED VIEW

MATERIALS LIST (FINISHED DIMENSIONS)

Parts

Case

A. Sides (2)   ½″ x 5½″ x 35½″
B. Top/bottom (2) ½″ x 5½″ x 12″
C. Middle shelf   ¾″ x 1½″ x 12″
D. Back*   ¼″ x 12″ x 33″
E. Clock board*   ¼″ x 12″ x 13″
F. Chime mount   1½″ x 2″ x 2¾″
G. Sound hole
   frames* (2)   ¼″ x 2¾″ x 5¾″
H. Top/bottom
   spacers (2)   ½″ x 1½″ x 12½″
J. Middle spacer ½″ x ¾″ x 12½″

Base

K. Base front   ¾″ x 3½″ x 14″
L. Base front
   molding   ¼″ x 2¾″ x 14½″
M. Base sides (2) ¾″ x 3½″ x 6¾″
N. Base side
   moldings (2)   ¼″ x 2¾″ x 7″
P. Base cleats (2)   ½″ x ½″ x 6″

Waist molding

Q. Waist front
   molding   ¾″ x ¾″ x 14″
R. Waist side
   moldings (2)   ¾″ x ¾″ x 6¾″

Bonnet

S. Bonnet front ⅜″ x 5½″ x 13¼″
T. Bonnet sides (2) ⅜″ x 2″ x 6⅜″
U. Front bead
   molding   ¼″ x ⁷⁄₁₆″ x 13¾″
V. Side bead
   moldings (2)   ¼″ x ⁷⁄₁₆″ x 6⅝″
W. Bonnet front
   spacers (2)   ⅛″ x 4⅝″ x 5⅞″
X. Gooseneck
   moldings (2)   ⅝″ x 4¼″ x 6⅜″
Y. Bonnet side
   spacers (2)   ⅛″ x 1¼″ x 6½″
Z. Side cove
   moldings (2)   ⅝″ x ⅞″ x 7⅛″
AA. Finial post   ⅝″ x 1″ x 1¾″
BB. Finial cap   ¼″ x ¾″ x ¾″
CC. Bonnet cleats (2) ¼″ x ½″ x 6″

Doors

DD. Hood door
   stiles (2)   ½″ x 1½″ x 12½″
EE. Waist door
   stiles (2)   ½″ x 1½″ x 19¼″
FF. Door rails (4)   ½″ x 1½″ x 11″

* Make these parts from plywood.

Hardware

#6 x 1″ Flathead wood screws (12)
#6 x ¾″ Flathead wood screws (4)
#2 x ¼″ Roundhead wood screws
   (4)
⅜″ x 1¾″ Knife hinges and
   mounting screws (4 sets)
½″ Brass pulls (2)
Brass hook-and-eye latches (2)
Glass (⅛″ x 10¼″ x 10¼″ piece)
Glass (⅛″ x 10¼″ x 17″ piece)
Speaker cloth (8″ x 8″ piece)
14-day Spring-driven clockworks
   (with bim-bam chimes and
   22½″ pendulum)
9½″ diameter Shaker clock dial
Shaker clock hands
3″ Spire-and-ball finial

WHERE TO FIND IT

Order the knife hinges (#16C62), pulls (#02U22), movement (#3301X), dial (#7416S), and hands (#4970X) from:

Woodcraft Supply Corporation
210 Wood County Industrial Park
P. O. Box 1686
Parkersburg, WV 26102

Be sure to ask to have the winding-key holes punched in the dial. Order the finial (#38012) from:

Klockit
P.O. Box 636
Lake Geneva, WI 53147

PLAN OF PROCEDURE

1 Select the stock and cut the parts. Before beginning this project, order the movement, dial, and hands. Cut a scrap of ¼-inch plywood to about the same size as the dial, drill a hole to accommodate the hand shafts (on which the clock hands are mounted), and attach the movement to it temporarily. Secure the board in a vise or clamp it to a shelf and attach the pendulum. Wind up the movement and set the pendulum in motion. Measure the length of the pendulum (from the shaft to the center of the bob), its swing (side-to-side motion), and the dimensions of the movement. Check that the movement and pendulum will fit in the case as it's designed. If not, adjust the dimensions as necessary. When you've finished, put the movement in a plastic bag to protect it from dust.

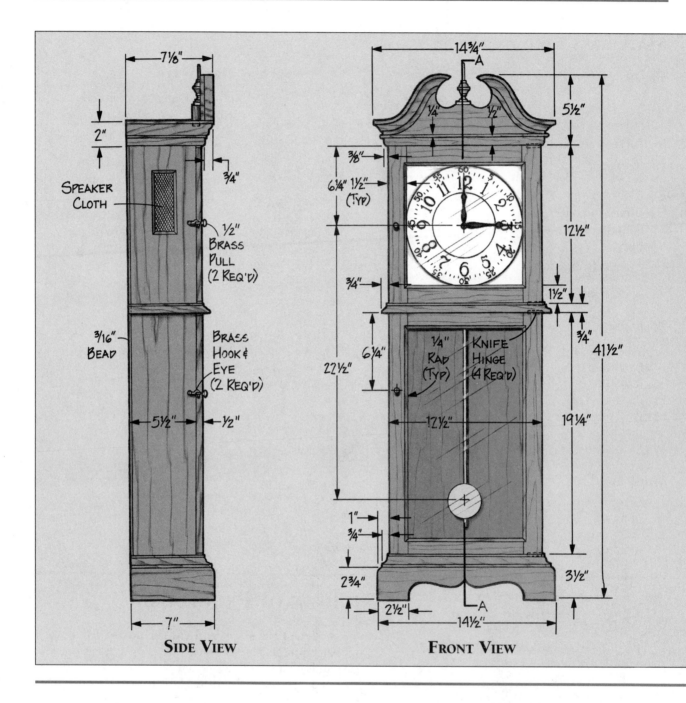

SIDE VIEW   **FRONT VIEW**

As designed, you can build this case from about 10 board feet of 4/4 (four-quarters) lumber and a 2-foot by 4-foot piece of ¼-inch plywood. You can use any cabinet hardwood; the clock shown is made from mahogany and mahogany-veneer plywood. Mahogany was the preferred wood among craftsmen who made Chippendale-style furniture during the last half of the eighteenth century. However, they also used walnut, cherry, and — less frequently — figured maple.

Decide which boards you will use to make specific parts. Resaw those boards that will be used to make ⅜-inch, ¼-inch, and ⅛-inch-thick parts. Plane the lumber to the thicknesses required, then cut the case parts to size. Glue up two ¾-inch-thick pieces to make the 1½-inch-thick chime mount. Do *not* cut the parts for the base, waist molding, bonnet, or doors yet — wait until after you have assembled the case. The dimensions specified may change slightly.

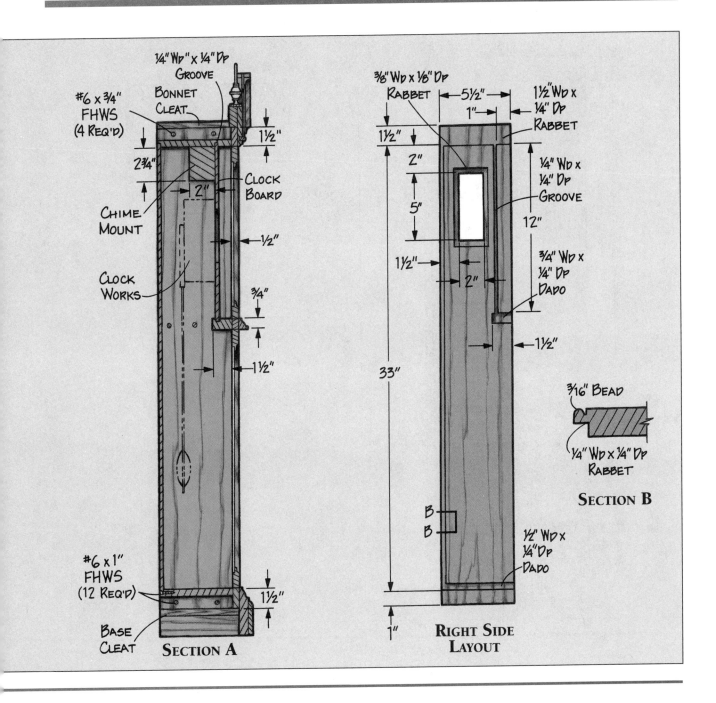

¼" WD" x ¼" DP GROOVE

BONNET CLEAT

#6 x ¾" FHWS (4 REQ'D)

1½"

2¾"

2"

CLOCK BOARD

CHIME MOUNT

CLOCK WORKS

½"

¾"

1½"

#6 x 1" FHWS (12 REQ'D)

1½"

BASE CLEAT

SECTION A

⅜" WD x ⅛" DP RABBET

5½"

1"

1½" WD x ¼" DP RABBET

1½"

2"

5"

¼" WD x ¼" DP GROOVE

12"

¾" WD x ¼" DP DADO

1½"

2"

1½"

33"

B

B

½" WD x ¼" DP DADO

3/16" BEAD

¼" WD x ¼" DP RABBET

SECTION B

1"

RIGHT SIDE LAYOUT

2 **Cut the joinery and beads in the case parts.**
Lay out the sides, as shown in the *Right Side Layout.*
Remember that each side is a mirror image of the
other. With a router or a dado cutter, make:

■ 1½-inch-wide, ¼-inch-deep rabbets in the top
ends of the sides to create a ledge for the top

■ A ¾-inch-wide, ¼-inch-deep blind dado to hold
the middle shelf

■ ½-inch-wide, ¼-inch-deep dadoes in the sides to
hold the bottom

■ ¼-inch-wide, ¼-inch-deep grooves in the sides,
top, and middle shelf to hold the clock board

■ ¼-inch-wide, ¼-inch-deep rabbets in the back
edges of the sides, top, and bottom to hold the back

■ 3/16-inch diameter beads near the back edges of
the sides

3 **Cut holes in the clock board.** Using a hole saw,
cut a 3-inch-diameter hole in the clock board, as
shown in the *Case/Front View.* This serves as an access

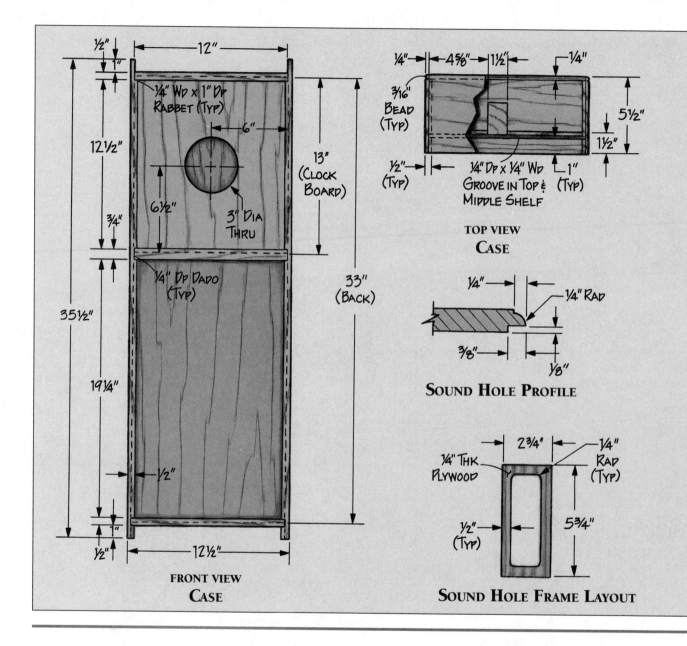

hole for the hand shafts and the winding keys. **Note:** If you've purchased a different movement from the one specified in the Materials List, it may require a different size access hole.

Temporarily attach the dial to the front of the clock board with small roundhead wood screws, one in each corner. Hold the movement in place on the back of the board, centering the hand shafts and the winding key posts inside the appropriate holes in the dial. Mark the location of the movement and set it aside. Remove the dial from the clock board and drill mounting holes in the clock board to hold the movement.

Place the movement in a plastic bag to protect it from dust, then put the movement, dial, and hands in a safe place until you have completed the case.

4 Cut the sound holes in the sides. Lay out the sound holes in the sides, as shown in the *Right Side Layout*. Cut the holes with a scroll saw or coping saw, then sand the sawed edges. Round over the edges of the sound holes on the outside surfaces, as shown in the *Sound Hole Profile*. Square the corners of this roundover with a carving chisel, making it look as if the sound holes were framed with quarter-round moldings. (*SEE FIGURE 8-1.*)

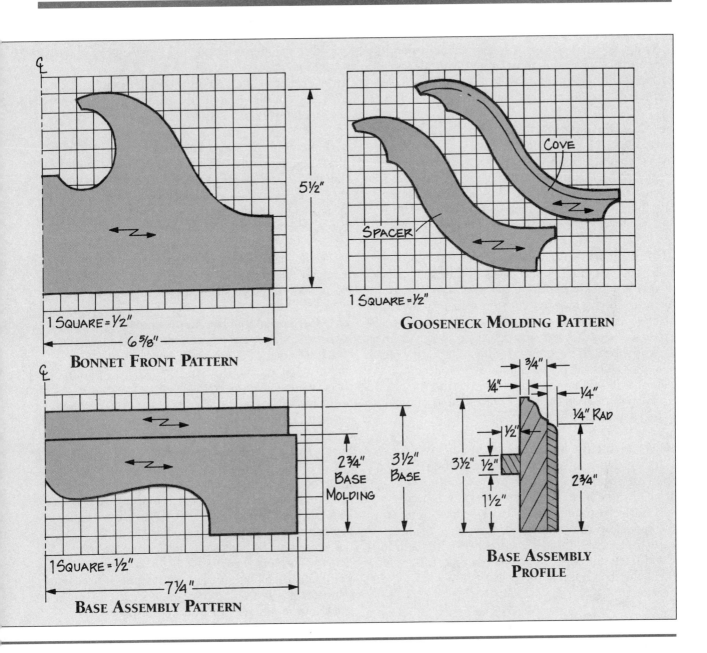

BONNET FRONT PATTERN

1 SQUARE = ½"

5½"

6⅝"

GOOSENECK MOLDING PATTERN

COVE

SPACER

1 SQUARE = ½"

BASE ASSEMBLY PATTERN

1 SQUARE = ½"

7¼"

2¾" BASE MOLDING

3½" BASE

BASE ASSEMBLY PROFILE

¾"

¼"

¼"

½"

3½"

½"

1½"

¼" RAD

2¾"

8-1 After rounding over the inside edges of the sound hole, square the corners with carving chisels. The completed sound holes should look as if they were lined with quarter-round moldings, mitered at the corners.

Rout a ⅜-inch-wide, ⅛-inch-deep rabbet around the perimeter of the sound holes on the inside surfaces. Square the corners of the rabbets with a chisel. (These rabbets will hold the sound hole frames.)

5 Make the base stock. Cut two boards 30 inches long, one ¾ inch by 3½ inches and the other ¼ inch by 2¾ inches. Using a router or a shaper, cut an ogee in the top edge of the ¾-inch-thick board. Round over the top edge of the other board. Glue the two boards face to face with the bottom edges flush to create the shape shown in the *Base Assembly Profile*.

6 Cut the base parts. Temporarily assemble the sides, top, bottom, bottom spacer, middle shelf, clock board, and back. Secure the back with #6 x 1-inch flathead wood screws, and the remaining parts with clamps. Make sure the case is square, then measure its dimensions — they may have changed slightly from what is shown in the drawings. Using these new measurements, cut the base front and sides to length, mitering the adjoining corners. Lay out the *Base Assembly Pattern* on the base front assembly and cut it with a band saw or scroll saw.

7 Assemble the base. Finish sand the base parts. With the clock case assembled, glue the bottom spacer to the bottom, but *don't* glue it to the sides. Then glue the base front assembly to the bottom spacer, the base side assemblies to the base front, and the base cleats to the base sides. *Don't* glue the base sides to the sides. Instead, secure them with flathead wood screws, driving the screws from inside the case. Make the shaft holes in the sides slightly oversize. (*SEE FIGURE 8-2.*)

8 Make the waist moldings. Cut a piece ¾ inch thick, 2 or more inches wide, and 30 inches long. In one edge, cut an ogee in the top arris and round over the bottom arris to create the shape shown in the *Waist Molding Profile*. Rip the molding from the shaped edge, and cut the waist moldings to length, mitering the adjoining ends.

9 Assemble the waist molding. Finish sand the waist molding parts. With the clock case assembled, glue the middle spacer to the middle shelf, but *don't* glue it to the sides. Glue the front waist molding to the spacer, then glue the side waist moldings to the front molding. Secure the side moldings to the sides with screws, driving the screws from inside the case.

Like the base assembly, the waist assembly is removable. Remove the screws and the top, slide the clock board up, then slide the assembly forward.

10 Cut and shape the bonnet parts. Cut two strips of wood, one ¼ x 2 x 30 inches, and the other ⅝ x 2 x 16 inches. Round over one edge of the ¼-inch-thick stock and rip a ⁷⁄₁₆-inch-wide strip from the shaped edge to make the bead moldings. Cut a ½-inch-radius cove in one edge of the ⅝-inch-thick stock, then rip a ⅞-inch-wide strip from the shaped edge to make the side cove moldings, as shown in the *Bonnet Molding Profiles*.

Cut the bonnet parts to size, cutting the bonnet front, bonnet sides, side spacers, side moldings, and front bead molding about ½ inch longer than specified. Lay out the patterns of the bonnet front, bonnet front spacers, and gooseneck moldings, as shown in the *Bonnet Front Pattern* and the *Gooseneck Molding Pattern*. Then cut them with a band saw or scroll saw. Round over the bottom edges of the bonnet front and bonnet sides, and rout ½-inch-radius coves in the front cove moldings. (*SEE FIGURE 8-3.*) Also rout ¼-inch-wide, ³⁄₁₆-inch-deep grooves in the bonnet front and sides to hold the bead moldings.

8-2 Although the base is secured to the case with screws, it isn't permanently attached. You can remove the base and the bottom from it by loosening the screws in the sides and the back, then sliding the assembly forward. The waist and bonnet assemblies are made in the same manner. This "knock-down" design will come in handy when you hang the doors.

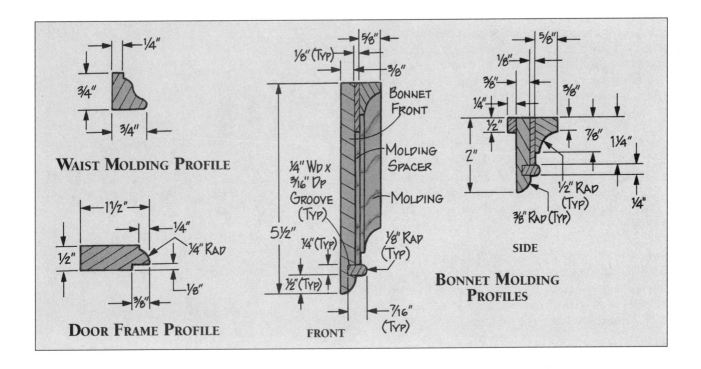

WAIST MOLDING PROFILE

DOOR FRAME PROFILE

FRONT

BONNET MOLDING PROFILES

SIDE

BONNET FRONT

MOLDING SPACER

MOLDING

11 **Assemble the bonnet.** Glue together the bonnet sides, side spacers, side cove moldings, and side bead moldings, as shown in the *Bonnet Molding Profiles/Side.* Also glue together the bonnet front, front spacers, gooseneck moldings, and front bead molding, as shown in the *Bonnet Molding Profiles/Front.* Miter the adjoining ends of the bonnet molding assemblies.

Finish sand the bonnet parts and assemblies. Glue the bonnet front molding assembly, front spacer, finial post, and finial cap together, then glue the side molding assemblies and the bonnet cleats to the front assembly. Attach the assembled bonnet to the case

sides with #6 x ¾-inch flathead wood screws, and install the finial on top of the finial post and cap.

12 **Cut the door parts and door joinery.** Measure the door openings on the front of the case. Cut the door parts, adjusting the dimensions as necessary. Rout mortises in the door stiles and matching tenons in the ends of the rails, as shown in the *Door Joinery Detail.* Round the edges of the tenon.

13 **Assemble the doors.** Finish sand the stiles and rails, then glue them together. When the glue dries,

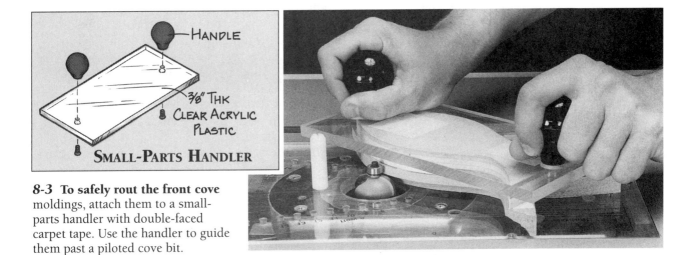

HANDLE

⅜" THK CLEAR ACRYLIC PLASTIC

SMALL-PARTS HANDLER

8-3 To safely rout the front cove moldings, attach them to a small-parts handler with double-faced carpet tape. Use the handler to guide them past a piloted cove bit.

round over the edges of the doors on the outside surfaces, as shown in the *Door Frame Profile*. Square the corners of this roundover with a carving chisel, just as you did when making the sound holes. Rout a ⅜-inch-wide, ⅛-inch-deep rabbet around the inside edges of the doors. Square the corners of the rabbets with a chisel. (These rabbets will hold the glass.)

14 **Hang the doors.** Fit the doors to the openings. The outside edges of the stiles must be flush with the sides, and there should be a ¹⁄₃₂- to ¹⁄₁₆-inch gap between the rails and the spacers at the tops and bottoms of the doors.

Cut mortises in the case and the doors for the knife hinges, then install the leaves of the hinges in the mortises. To hang the doors, remove the base, waist, and bonnet from the case. Then replace them, inserting the hinge pins in their pivot holes as you reassemble the case. Install a pull and a latch on each door.

15 **Install the movement and chimes.** Remove the top and the clock board from the case. Attach the movement to the clock board and secure the chimes to the chime mount. Slide the clock board into the case and temporarily stick the chime mount to it with double-faced carpet tape, aligning the chimes with the hammers in the works. Install the pendulum, wind the clock, and test the chimes. If the chimes sound light and indistinct, they may be too far away from the hammers. If the sound is dead and flat, they're too close. When you're certain the chimes are properly placed, glue the chime mount to the clock board permanently.

16 **Finish the case.** Remove the movement and chimes from the case, cover them, and store them in a clean place. Take the case apart, detach all the hardware, and set it aside. Do any necessary touch-up sanding and apply a finish.

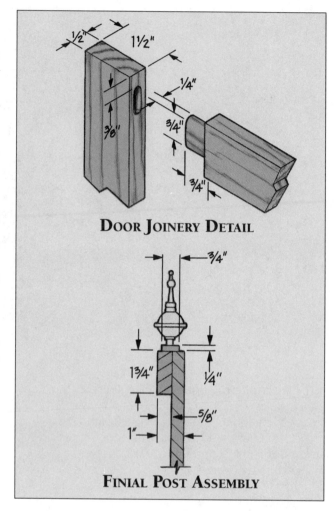

DOOR JOINERY DETAIL

FINIAL POST ASSEMBLY

> ☞ **FOR BEST RESULTS**
>
> Let the case sit for at least a week before rubbing out the finish and replacing the movement. The fumes from a new finish may corrode the delicate metal parts, especially if the movement is made of brass.

17 **Reassemble the clock.** Install the glass in the doors with silicone caulk — lay a tiny bead around the rabbet, then press the glass in place. When the

caulk dries, the panes will be permanently secured. Let any squeeze-out dry 1 to 2 hours, then trim it away with a sharp knife.

Put the case back together. Cut away the interior of small pieces of plywood to make the sound hole frames, as shown in the *Sound Hole Frame Layout*. Cover the frames with speaker cloth, using wood glue to adhere the cloth to the plywood. Then install the frames in the rabbets around the inside edges of the sound holes. This should be a "press fit;" friction will hold them in place. If they seem loose, secure them with small screws.

Attach the dial, movement, and chimes to the clock board assembly, slide the clock board into the case, and cover it with the top. Attach the pendulum, wind the clock, and set the pendulum in motion. For several weeks, check carefully to see whether the clock gains or loses time. If it's fast, lower the bob on the pendulum slightly. If it's slow, raise the bob.

9

MISSION BOOKCASE

Mission-style furniture appeared around the turn of the twentieth century, a product of the Arts and Crafts movement. Mission craftsmen rejected the excessive ornamentation of the Victorian era and made unpretentious, functional furniture such as this bookcase (A). Often, they used joinery as one of their few decorative elements. On this piece, for example, the pegged through mortise-and-tenon joints add visual interest.

Oak was the preferred wood of Mission craftsmen. Accordingly, this bookcase was built from quarter-sawn white oak. The "silver grain" (rays) made visible by quarter-sawing help to dress up an otherwise simple design. Unfortunately, these rays are so prominent that when you put them next to a piece of plain-sawn oak (showing flat grain), the difference is jarring. This created a problem when we assembled the case for the first time.

An oak board that's cut to show silver grain on its face will show flat grain at the edge. This was the case with the front corner posts, and because of their prominent position in the case, the difference between the surfaces was immediately noticeable. To solve this problem, we remade the corner posts in three pieces, mitering the corners so the rays show on all outside surfaces (B).

We ran into another problem when we added the shelves. On most bookcases, the sides are solid boards that expand and contract in the same direction as the shelves. You can attach the shelves to the sides with no ill effect. But on this project, the sides are frame-and-panel assemblies. Although the panel moves, the frame does not. Consequently, we had to attach the shelves at the front corners *only*. The back corners float in dadoes, which allows them to move.

A

B

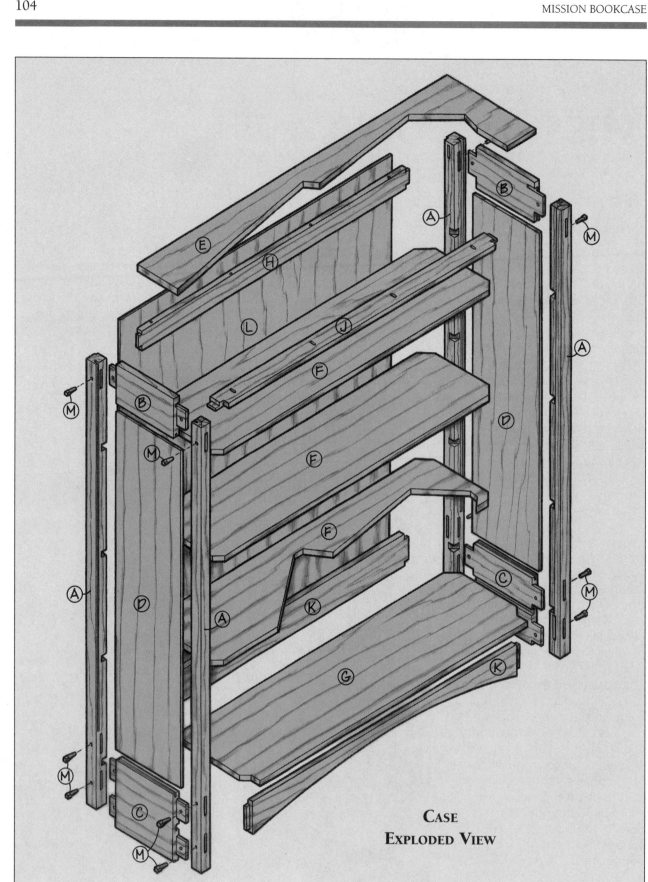

CASE
EXPLODED VIEW

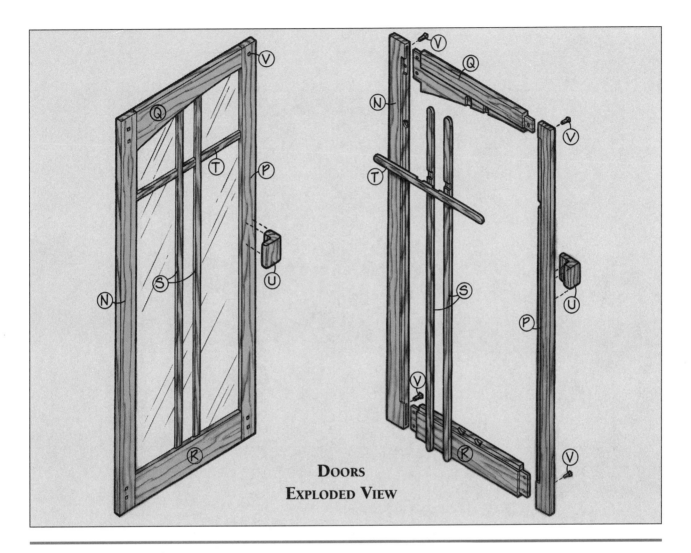

Doors
Exploded View

Materials List (FINISHED DIMENSIONS)

Parts

A. Legs* (4)   1½″ x 1½″ x 58¼″

B. Top side rails (2)   ¾″ x 5″ x 12¼″

C. Bottom side rails (2)   ¾″ x 8¾″ x 12¼″

D. Side panels (2)   ¼″ x 10″ x 44″

E. Top   ¾″ x 14″ x 49″

F. Shelves (3)   ¾″ x 10⅞″ x 44″

G. Bottom   ¾″ x 12⅜″ x 44″

H. Back top cleat   ¾″ x 2¼″ x 43″

J. Front top cleat   ¾″ x 2¼″ x 44¼″

K. Bottom cleat/rail (2)   ¾″ x 4″ x 43″

L. Back†   ¼″ x 43″ x 52¾″

M. Long pegs (12)   ¼″ x ¼″ x 1⅛″

N. Outside door stiles (2)   ¾″ x 2½″ x 52″

P. Inside door stiles (2)   ¾″ x 2″ x 52″

Q. Top door rails (2)   ¾″ x 5″ x 19½″

R. Bottom door rails (2)   ¾″ x 4″ x 19½″

S. Vertical glazing bars (4)   ⅜″ x ¾″ x 46½″

T. Horizontal glazing bars (2)   ⅜″ x ¾″ x 17½″

U. Door pulls (2)   1½″ x 2¼″ x 3″

V. Short pegs (14)   ¼″ x ¼″ x ¾″

Hardware

#8 x ¾″ Flathead wood screws (16)

#10 x 1¼″ Flathead wood screws (8)

#10 x 1½″ Roundhead wood screws (4)

1½″ x 2½″ Butt hinges and mounting screws (4 sets)

Magnetic door latches and mounting screws (2)

⅛″ x 17⅜″ x 46⅜″ Glass panels (2)

* The front legs may be glued up from several pieces of wood.
† Make the back from plywood.

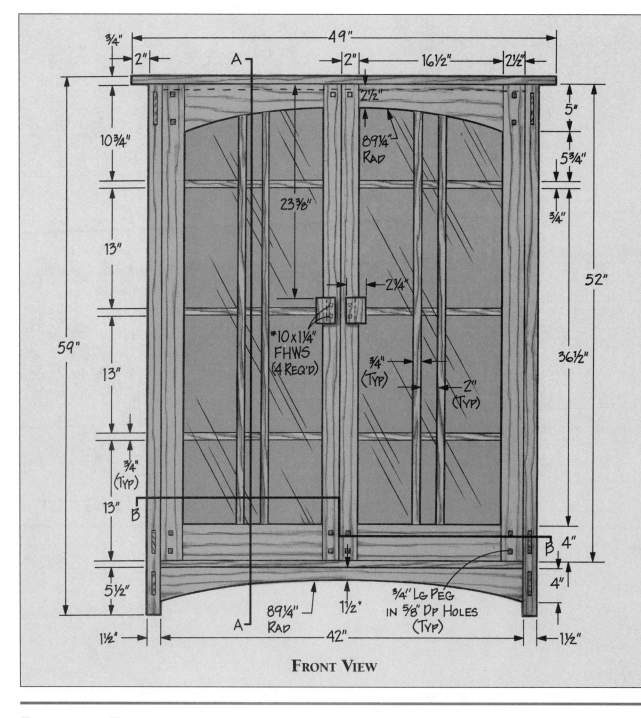

FRONT VIEW

PLAN OF PROCEDURE

1 **Select the stock and cut the parts.** To make this project, you need approximately 38 board feet of 4/4 (four-quarters) stock, 8 board feet of 8/4 (eight-quarters) stock, and a sheet of ¼-inch plywood. Mission craftsmen used mahogany and several domestic hardwoods, but they preferred oak. The

bookcase shown is made from white oak and red oak-veneer plywood. (The slight color difference between white and red oak isn't noticeable once the wood is stained.)

Select the 4/4 stock you want to use for the side panels, resaw the boards, and plane them to ¼ inch

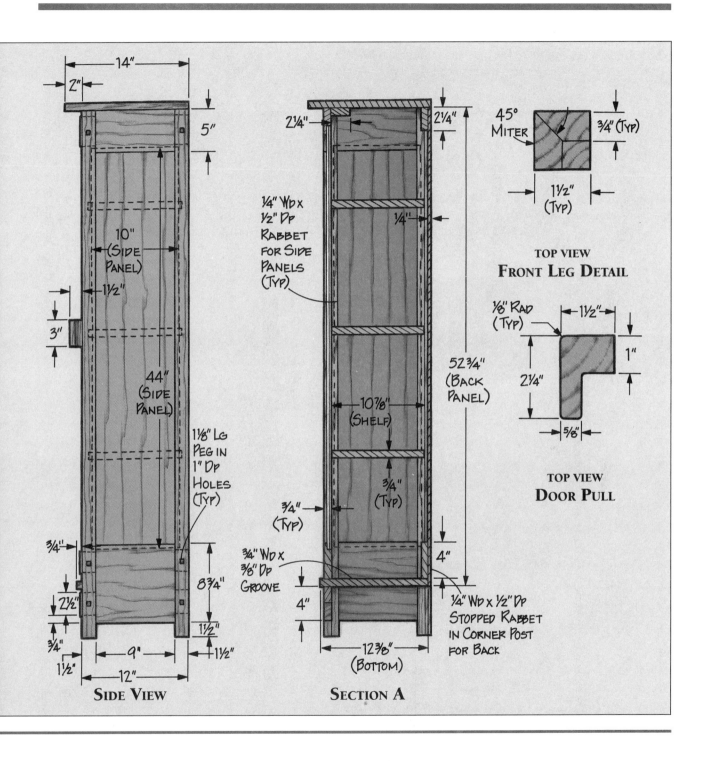

14"

2"

5"

10"
(SIDE
PANEL)

1½"

3"

44"
(SIDE
PANEL)

1⅛" LG
PEG IN
1" DP
HOLES
(TYP)

¾"

8¾"

2½"

¾"

1½"

9"

1½"

12"

SIDE VIEW

2¼"

2¼"

¼" WD X
½" DP
RABBET
FOR SIDE
PANELS
(TYP)

¼"

52¾"
(BACK
PANEL)

10⅞"
(SHELF)

¾"
(TYP)

¾"
(TYP)

4"

4"

4"

¾" WD X
⅜" DP
GROOVE

¼" WD X ½" DP
STOPPED RABBET
IN CORNER POST
FOR BACK

12⅜"
(BOTTOM)

SECTION A

45°
MITER

¾" (TYP)

1½"
(TYP)

TOP VIEW
FRONT LEG DETAIL

⅛" RAD
(TYP)

1½"

1"

2¼"

⅝"

TOP VIEW
DOOR PULL

thick. Plane the remaining 4/4 lumber to ¾ inch thick and the 8/4 lumber to 1½ inches thick. If you're using rift-sawn or quarter-sawn lumber and you'd like the grain pattern to show on all surfaces of the legs, you'll need 2 extra board feet of 4/4 lumber and 2 board feet less of 8/4 lumber. Glue up the front leg stock from

¾-inch-thick stock, as shown in the *Front Leg Detail/Top View*.

Cut the case parts to the sizes given in the Materials List. Do *not* cut the door parts yet; wait until after you have built the case.

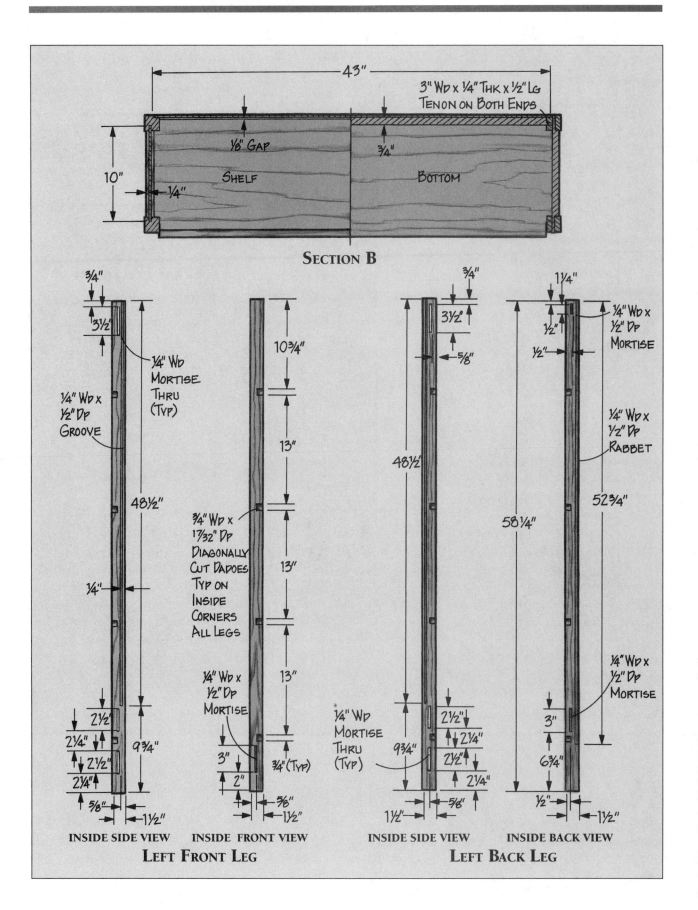

43"

3" Wd x ¼" Thk x ½" Lg
Tenon on Both Ends

⅛" Gap

¾"

10"

Shelf   Bottom

¼"

Section B

¾"

3½"

¼" Wd
Mortise
Thru
(Typ)

¼" Wd x
½" Dp
Groove

48½"

¼"

10¾"

13"

¾" Wd x
1⁷⁄₃₂" Dp
Diagonally
Cut Dadoes
Typ on
Inside
Corners
All Legs

13"

13"

¼" Wd x
½" Dp
Mortise

2½"
2¼"
2½"
2¼"

9¾"

5⁄8"

1½"

3"

2"

5⁄8"

1½"

¾" (Typ)

¾"

3½"

5⁄8"

1¼"

½"

½"

¼" Wd x
½" Dp
Mortise

¼" Wd x
½" Dp
Rabbet

48½"

58¼"

52¾"

¼" Wd
Mortise
Thru
(Typ)

9¾"

2½"
2¼"
2½"
2¼"

1½"

5⁄8"

3"

6¾"

½"

1½"

¼" Wd x
½" Dp
Mortise

INSIDE SIDE VIEW   **INSIDE FRONT VIEW**   **INSIDE SIDE VIEW**   **INSIDE BACK VIEW**

Left Front Leg   **Left Back Leg**

2 Cut the joinery in the legs. Lay out the joinery on the legs, as shown in the *Left Front Leg* and *Left Back Leg* drawings. Remember that the right legs are mirror images of the left ones. When the legs are clearly marked, cut these joints:

■ ¼-inch-wide, 3½-inch-long through mortises in the inside surfaces of the legs to hold the top side rails

■ ¼-inch-wide, 2½-inch-long through mortises in the inside side surfaces of the legs to hold the bottom side rails

■ ¼-inch-wide, ½-inch-deep, 3-inch-long mortises in the inside front surfaces of the front legs to hold the bottom front rail, and in the inside back surface of the back legs to hold the bottom back cleat

■ ¼-inch-wide, ½-inch-deep, 1¼-inch-long mortises in the inside back surfaces of the back legs to hold the top back cleat

■ ¼-inch-wide, ½-inch-deep, 48½-inch-long blind grooves in the inside side surfaces of the legs to hold the side panels

■ ¼-inch-wide, ½-inch-deep, 52¾-inch-long blind rabbets in the inside back surfaces of the back legs to hold the back.

To cut the diagonal dadoes that hold the shelves, make a V-jig and attach it to your miter gauge. Rest the legs in the V-jig as you cut or rout the dadoes. (*See* Figure 9-1.)

3 Cut the joinery in the rails and cleats. Lay out the tenons, mortises, and grooves on the rails and cleats. Remember that the left and right side rails are mirror images of each other. When the parts are clearly marked, cut or rout these joints:

■ ¾-inch-wide, ⅜-inch-deep grooves in the inside surfaces of the bottom side rails to hold the bottom, as shown in the *Right Bottom Side Rail/Inside Side View*

■ ¼-inch-wide, ½-inch-deep, 1½-inch-long mortises on the inside faces of the top side rails to hold the top front cleats, as shown in the *Right Top Side Rail/Inside Side View*

■ ¼-inch-wide, ½-inch-deep grooves in the bottom edges of the top side rails and the top edges of the bottom side rails to hold the side panels, as shown on the *Right Top Side Rail/Bottom View* and *Right Bottom Side Rail/Top View*

■ ¼-inch-thick, 1⅝-inch-long, 3½-inch-wide tenons on the ends of the top side rails

■ ¼-inch-thick, 1⅝-inch-long, 2½-inch-wide tenons on the ends of the bottom side rails

■ ¼-inch-thick, ½-inch-long, 1½-inch-wide tenons on the ends of the front top cleat, as shown in the *Front Top Cleat Layout*

■ ¼-inch-thick, ½-inch-long, 1¼-inch-wide tenons on the ends of the back top cleat, as shown in the *Back Top Cleat Layout*

■ ¼-inch-thick, ½-inch-long, 3-inch-wide tenons on the ends of the back bottom cleat and front bottom rail, as shown in the *Back Bottom Cleat Layout* and *Front Bottom Rail Layout*

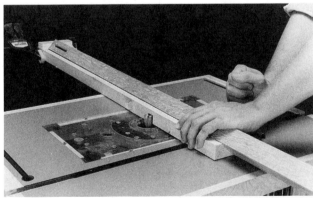

9-1 The shelves rest in ¾-inch-wide, ¹⁷/₃₂-inch-deep *diagonal* dadoes in the inside corners of the legs. To cut these dadoes, first make the V-jig and stop shown and attach it to your miter gauge. Position the stop to cut the first set of dadoes and secure it to the V-jig. Rest a leg in the jig, inside corner down, and cut through both the jig and the leg. Make the same cut in the other three legs, reposition the stop, and repeat for the next set of dadoes. Continue until you have cut all the diagonal dadoes in all the legs.

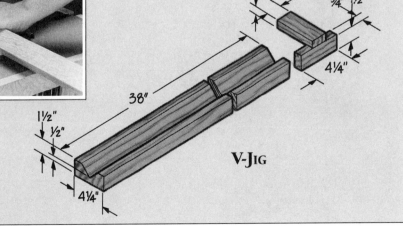

V-Jig

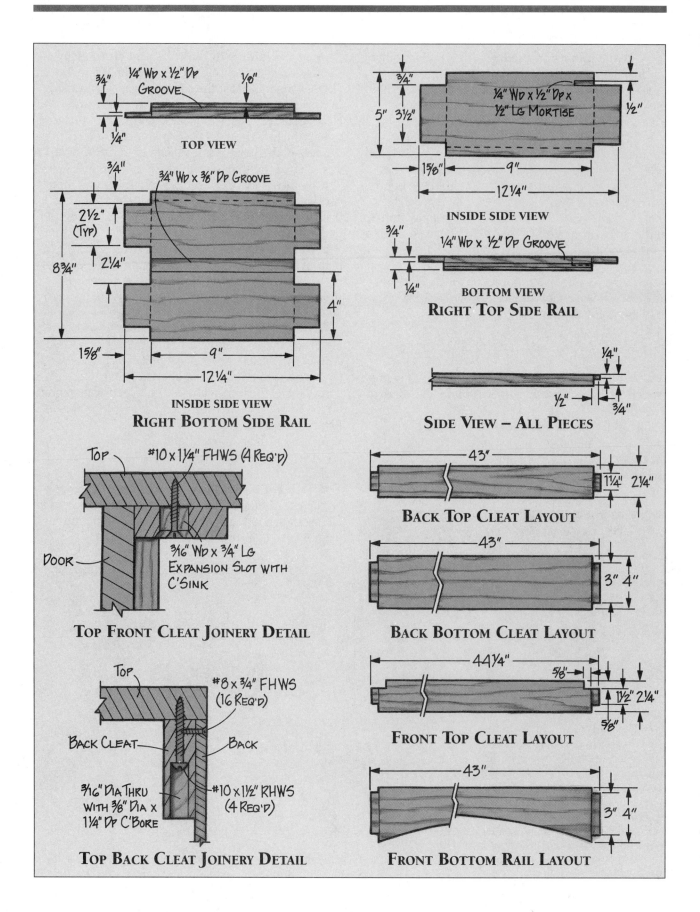

¼" WD x ½" DP GROOVE

¾"

⅛"

¼"

TOP VIEW

¾"

¾" WD x ⅜" DP GROOVE

2½" (TYP)

2¼"

8¾"

4"

1⅝"

9"

12¼"

INSIDE SIDE VIEW
RIGHT BOTTOM SIDE RAIL

¾"

¼" WD x ½" DP x ½" LG MORTISE

5"   3½"

½"

1⅝"   9"

12¼"

INSIDE SIDE VIEW

¾"

¼" WD x ½" DP GROOVE

¼"

BOTTOM VIEW
RIGHT TOP SIDE RAIL

¼"

½"   ¾"

SIDE VIEW – ALL PIECES

43"

1¼"   2¼"

BACK TOP CLEAT LAYOUT

43"

3"   4"

BACK BOTTOM CLEAT LAYOUT

44¼"   ⅝"

1½"   2¼"

⅝"

FRONT TOP CLEAT LAYOUT

43"

3"   4"

FRONT BOTTOM RAIL LAYOUT

TOP

#10 x 1¼" FHWS (4 REQ'D)

DOOR

3/16" WD x ¾" LG EXPANSION SLOT WITH C'SINK

TOP FRONT CLEAT JOINERY DETAIL

TOP

#8 x ¾" FHWS (16 REQ'D)

BACK CLEAT   BACK

3/16" DIA THRU WITH ⅜" DIA x 1¼" DP C'BORE

#10 x 1½" RHWS (4 REQ'D)

TOP BACK CLEAT JOINERY DETAIL

4 Cut the profile of the front bottom rail. Using a beam compass, lay out the curved profile of the front bottom rail, as shown in the *Front View.* (*See Figure 9-2.*) Cut the curve with a band saw or a saber saw, then sand the sawed edge.

5 Cut the profiles of the front top cleat, shelves, and bottom. Lay out the notches on the ends of the front top cleat, as shown in the *Front Top Cleat Layout.* Also lay out the notches and mitered corners on the shelves and the bottom, as shown in the *Shelf/Bottom Layout.* Cut these profiles with a band saw or saber saw, then sand the sawed edges.

6 Make the holes and the slots in the top cleats. The top is secured to the top cleats with screws. Drill four ³⁄₁₆-inch-diameter holes with ³⁄₈-inch-diameter, 1¼-inch-deep counterbores in the edge of the top back cleat, as shown in the *Top Back Cleat Joinery*

Detail. Although the precise location of these holes isn't critical, they should be centered in the edge and evenly spaced along the length of the cleat.

Cut ³⁄₁₆-inch-wide, ³⁄₄-inch-long expansion slots with countersinks (beveled edges) in the face of the top front cleat, as shown in the *Top Front Cleat Joinery Detail.* These slots let the top expand and contract.

7 Assemble the case. Finish sand the parts of the case. Test fit all the joinery, and make any necessary adjustments. Finish the panels so raw wood won't show when they contract. Glue the legs and side rails together. As you do, slip the side panels into their grooves, but *don't* glue the panels in place. Let them float in their grooves. Let the glue dry, then sand the tenons in the back legs flush with the back surfaces. However, let the tenons in the front legs protrude slightly. Peg the tenons in their mortises. (*See Figures 9-3 through 9-5.*)

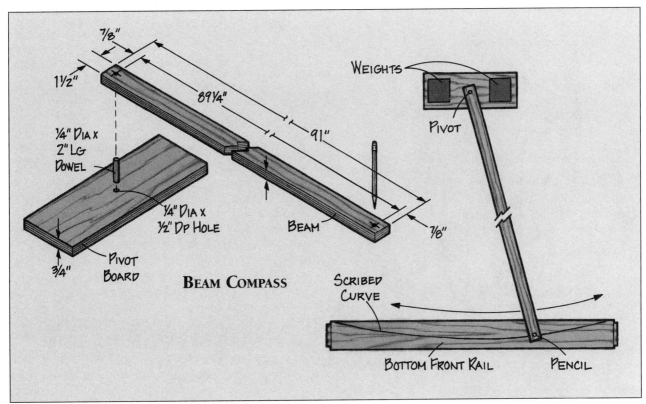

9-2 To scribe the curve on the front bottom rail, make a *beam compass* from a long scrap of wood. Cut a strip ¾ inch thick, 1½ inches wide, and 91 inches long to make the beam. Drill two ¼-inch-diameter holes through the thickness of the

beam, 89¼ inches apart. Drill another ¼-inch-diameter hole in a scrap of ¾-inch plywood and insert a ¼-inch-diameter, 2-inch-long dowel in the hole — this will serve as the pivot for the compass. Weight the pivot board down on your shop floor

and place one end of the beam over the dowel. Insert a pencil through the hole you drilled in the other end of the beam. Position the front bottom rail under the pencil-end of the beam and scribe the curve, swinging the beam around the pivot.

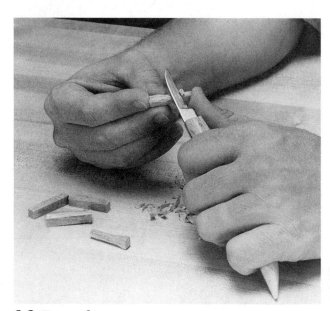

9-3 To peg the tenons, you must drive square pegs into round holes. Begin by whittling each peg so that it is more and more round toward one end. When you're finished, this end should be round and the other square. The square portion should be just ¼ to ½ inch long. Also chamfer the top edges, as shown in the *Peg Detail*.

9-4 Drill a hole, as big around as the peg is square, through the mortise and tenon. Using a small straight chisel or a parting tool (also called a V-groove chisel), carve the outside edge of the hole square.

9-5 Coat the peg with glue and drive it into the hole. Tap it in so the top is almost (but not quite) flush with the surface. (About ¹⁄₁₆ inch should protrude.) Be careful not to hit the peg so hard that it splinters.

Glue the side assemblies, shelves, bottom, cleats, and bottom rail together. Glue the shelves and the bottom to the *front legs only*. Let them float in the diagonal dadoes in the back legs and the grooves in the bottom side rails. This way, they can expand and contract independently of the case.

Attach the top to the case by driving wood screws through the top cleats. Attach the back with short flat-head wood screws, driving them through the back and into the legs and back cleats.

8 Cut the door parts. Measure the assembled case — the dimensions will probably have changed from what is shown in the drawings. Cut the door parts to fit the case, adjusting the dimensions as needed.

FOR BEST RESULTS

Make the doors to fill the opening, then sand or plane them to fit with a small gap all the way around the frames.

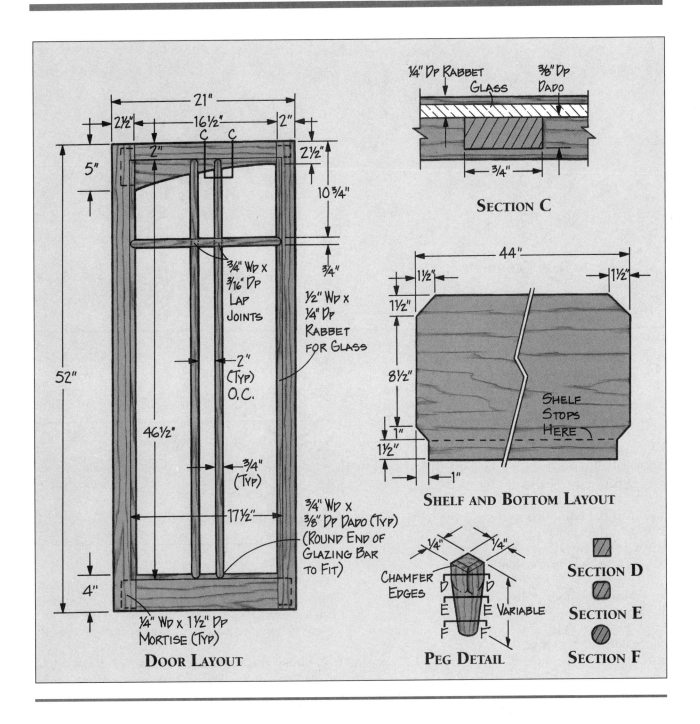

SECTION C

SHELF AND BOTTOM LAYOUT

DOOR LAYOUT

PEG DETAIL

SECTION D

SECTION E

SECTION F

9 **Cut the mortises, tenons, and rabbets.** Lay out the ¼-inch-wide, 1½-inch-deep mortises in the stiles, as shown in the *Door Layout*. Rout the mortises, then cut tenons on the ends of the rails to fit the mortises, as shown in the *Door Rail Tenon Detail*. Rout ½-inch-wide, ¼-inch-deep rabbets in the inside edges of the door stiles and bottom door rails, and 3-inch-wide, ¼-inch-deep rabbets in the top door rails. These rabbets will hold the glass panels in the doors.

10 **Cut the profiles of the top door rails.** Temporarily assemble the door frames. Lay the doors side by side on your shop floor. With the same shop-made beam compass you used to mark the bottom front rail, scribe the curves on the top door rails. Disassemble the door frames, cut the curves, and sand the sawed edges.

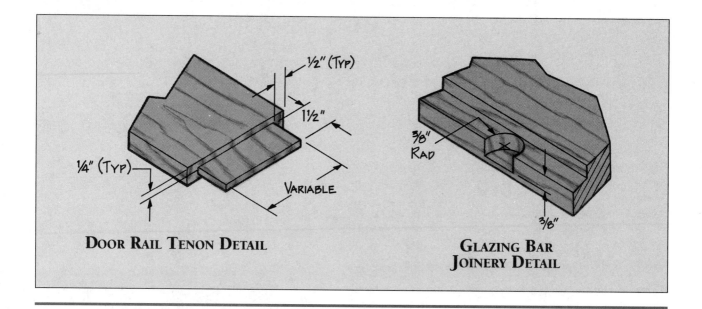

DOOR RAIL TENON DETAIL   **GLAZING BAR JOINERY DETAIL**

11 **Cut the dadoes in the rails and stiles for the glazing bars.** Each door has a decorative grid consisting of two vertical members and one horizontal member called *glazing bars*. These bars rest in ¾-inch-wide, ⅜-inch-deep round-end blind dadoes in the rails and stile. Rout the dadoes as shown in the *Glazing Bar Joinery Detail,* then round the ends of the glazing bars to fit the dadoes.

12 **Cut the lap joints in the glazing bars.** Where the horizontal and vertical glazing bars overlap, cut ¾-inch-wide, ³⁄₁₆-inch-deep dadoes in their faces. These will form lap joints.

13 **Make the door pulls.** Cut 1¼-inch-wide, ⅞-inch-deep rabbets in the back faces of the door pulls, as shown in the *Door Pull/Top View.* Round over all the corners and arrises *except* where the pulls are attached to the door frames.

14 **Assemble and hang the doors.** Finish sand the door parts, then glue the stiles, rails, and glazing bars together. Let the glue dry and install pegs in the corners to lock the tenons in the mortises.

Fit the doors to the opening, shaving down the outside edges until there's a small gap (about ¹⁄₁₆ inch wide) between the outside edges of the door frames and the case. There should also be a small gap between the doors.

Hang the doors from the front legs. On the bookcase shown, the doors swing on "no-mortise" hinges. These hinges have thin, nested leaves and don't have

to be mortised into the frame or the case. If you use ordinary butt hinges, you must cut hinge mortises.

WHERE TO FIND IT

You can buy no-mortise hinges from:
The Woodworkers' Store
21801 Industrial Boulevard
Rogers, MN 55374

When you're satisfied that the doors swing properly on their hinges, install the door pulls. Glue and screw them to the inside door stiles, as shown on the *Front View.* Install magnetic latches to keep the doors closed.

15 **Finish the bookcase.** Disassemble the doors, top, and back from the case. Remove the hinges, latches, and screws, and set them aside. Do any necessary touch-up sanding, then apply a finish to all wooden surfaces, inside and out. Rub out the finish with paste wax, then replace the top and back.

Install glass in the doors. Lay a small bead of clear silicone caulk in the glass rabbet, all around the inside of each door frame. Lay the glass in place, squeezing the caulk flat. Let the caulk dry 1 to 2 hours, then trim away any excess with a sharp knife. (The silicone caulk will secure the glass with no need of glass beads or glazing points.) Hang the doors and reinstall the latches.

10

ROUND TAVERN TABLE

Whenever you build a project with a wide expanse of solid wood, you confront *three* problems with wood movement. The first is obvious. Wood expands and contracts across the grain. The wider the board, the more the expansion and contraction. At 48 inches wide, you can expect this tabletop to move about ½ inch overall, depending on the wood used to make it.

The second is not as apparent, but it's just as important. When a board moves, it doesn't always stay flat. Wood showing flat grain generally cups in the opposite direction of the annual rings. Because of this, wide tabletops may not stay flat. Depending on how you assemble the top, it may tend to curl at the edges, raise in the middle, or develop "waves." You can prevent these problems by carefully

arranging the grain and employing some judicious bracework.

The third problem is much more subtle. When you glue boards edge to edge, you sometimes get *glue steps* — minuscule but noticeable changes in the surface level from one board to the next. This problem can also be avoided by arranging the wood grain properly.

Note: This table was designed by master craftsman David T. Smith.

Photo courtesy of *The Workshops of David T. Smith*, Morrow, Ohio

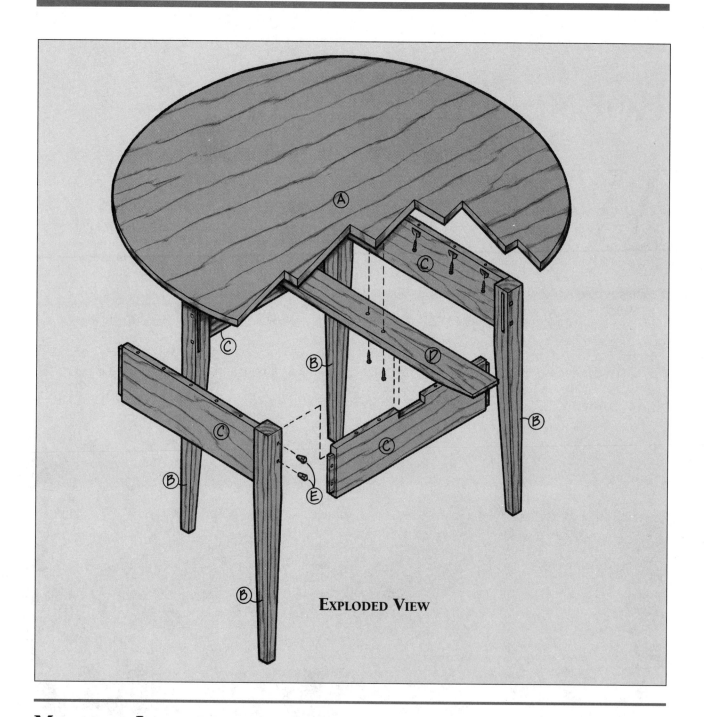

EXPLODED VIEW

MATERIALS LIST (FINISHED DIMENSIONS)

Parts

A. Top   48″ dia. x ¾″
B. Legs (4)   2″ x 2″ x 28¼″
C. Aprons (4)   ¾″ x 5″ x 25½″
D. Brace   ¾″ x 4″ x 44″
E. Pegs (16)   ⅜″ x ⅜″ x 1¼″

Hardware

#8 x 1¼″ Roundhead wood
  screws (18)

#8 x 1¼″ Flathead wood screws
  (12)

#8 x ¾″ Flathead wood screws
  (4)

#8 Flat washers (18)

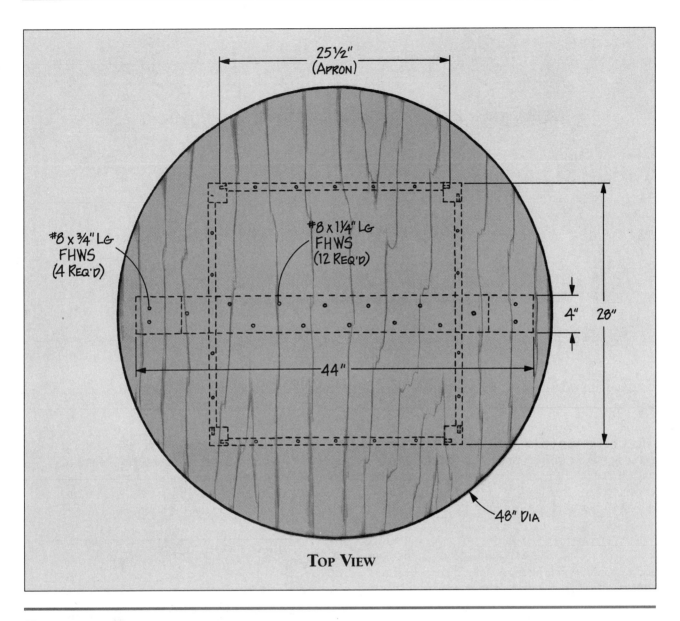

25½"
(APRON)

#8 x ¾" LG
FHWS
(4 REQ'D)

#8 x 1¼" LG
FHWS
(12 REQ'D)

4" 28"

44"

48" DIA

TOP VIEW

PLAN OF PROCEDURE

1 Select the stock and cut the parts. To make this table you need about 24 board feet of 4/4 (four-quarters) stock for the top, aprons, and brace; and 6 board feet of 10/4 (ten-quarters) stock for the legs. You might be able to get by with smaller leg stock if you can find a "strong" 8/4 — eight-quarters stock that's about ⅛ inch oversize. You can use almost any cabinet-grade hardwood — the table shown is made from maple.

Plane the leg stock to 2 inches thick and the 4/4 stock to ¾ inches thick. Cut the legs, aprons, and brace to size. Also cut the parts to make the top. Save the scraps to make the pegs.

2 Glue up the top. Carefully "read" the wood grain in the top boards before you glue them up. Do they show flat, quarter, or mixed grain on their faces? Which way do the growth rings cup? At what angle do the growth rings meet the edges?

Wood that shows flat or mixed grain on its face tends to cup in the *opposite* direction of the growth rings. If this is the case, glue the boards together with the growth rings curving *up*. The assembly will act like a single board, tending to curl under at the edges and rise in the middle. This tendency can be easily controlled by the brace, which will hold the top flat as it moves. The top may curl down slightly at the

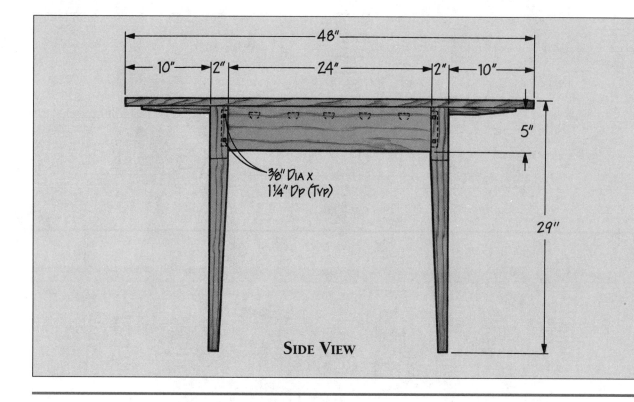

SIDE VIEW

edges, but it won't be that noticeable. If you turn the boards with the growth rings curving down, the top will curl up at the edges — this will be much more conspicuous.

Some craftsmen advise you to *alternate* the growth rings, turning one up, then one down, and so on. When you do this, the boards cup in opposite directions. The top may be wavy, but as long as the boards are narrow, it will look fairly flat. This is sound reasoning, and it makes sense when you are making a wide, *unsupported* panel, such as a table leaf.

But this method makes it more difficult to match the boards for color. When you turn the boards so all the rings curve up, you expose the maximum amount of heartwood, the most colorful part of the tree. When the rings curve down or alternate, you may have to deal with sapwood as well. (*SEE FIGURE 10-1.*)

You don't have to worry about any of this when the wood is quarter-sawn and the faces of the boards all show quarter grain. Quarter-sawn lumber has little tendency to cup, so the tabletop remains flat. It also expands and contracts less, so there isn't as much movement. (*SEE FIGURE 10-2.*)

Whether you use plain-sawn or quarter-sawn lumber, you should give some thought to the wood grain at the adjoining edges. Like the faces, the edges will show flat grain, quarter grain, or something in

between. Match the edges as well as possible, gluing quarter grain to quarter grain and flat grain to flat grain. If you glue quarter grain to flat grain, the two boards will expand and contract at different rates and a *glue step* will develop at the seam. (*SEE FIGURE 10-3.*)

TRY THIS TRICK

If possible, cut the pieces for the tabletop from a single board. "Fold" the pieces like a carpenter's rule, joining like edges. This has three advantages. First, it helps you match the grain on the edges, preventing the assembled tabletop from developing glue steps. Second, the grain will seem continuous because the pattern on the edges will be similar — it may be almost impossible to see the edge joints. And third, the color will be even because all the pieces are from the same board.

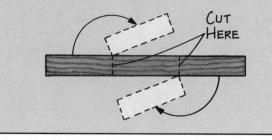

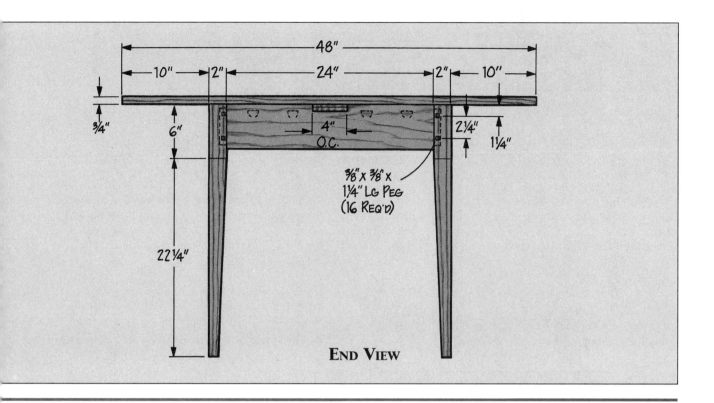

END VIEW

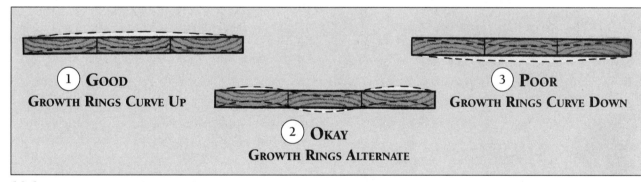

① GOOD
GROWTH RINGS CURVE UP

② OKAY
GROWTH RINGS ALTERNATE

③ POOR
GROWTH RINGS CURVE DOWN

10-1 How you orient the growth rings when you glue up a wide panel is a matter of some controversy. Some craftsmen (myself included) maintain that they should all curve up (1) because this exposes the maximum amount of heartwood. The color is more consistent, and the tendency for the panel to rise in the center is easily controlled by bracework. Others recommend you alternate the rings (2). The top will look generally flat, even though close inspection may show it's slightly wavy. However, this may expose a little sapwood, making it more difficult to match the colors. Most everyone agrees the worst arrangement is with the rings facing down (3). This exposes the most sapwood, and the panel may curl up at the edges.

10-2 Perhaps the best material for a tabletop, table leaf, or any other wide panel is *quarter-sawn* lumber. It expands and contracts only half as much as plain-sawn, and has little tendency to cup.

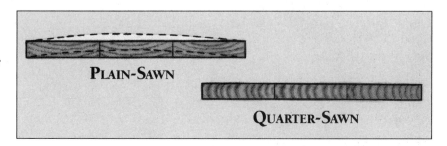

PLAIN-SAWN

QUARTER-SAWN

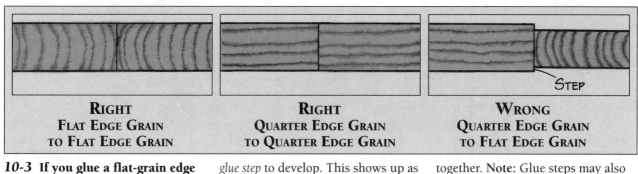

RIGHT
FLAT EDGE GRAIN
TO FLAT EDGE GRAIN

RIGHT
QUARTER EDGE GRAIN
TO QUARTER EDGE GRAIN

WRONG
QUARTER EDGE GRAIN
TO FLAT EDGE GRAIN

STEP

10-3 If you glue a flat-grain edge to a quarter-grain edge, the two boards will expand and contract at different rates. The glue will creep under the stress, allowing a small

glue step to develop. This shows up as an unsightly line at the seam between boards. To avoid these steps, carefully match the grain when deciding which edges to glue

together. **Note:** Glue steps may also develop if the boards don't have the same moisture content. Make sure the boards rest in your shop for several weeks before joining them.

Once you have arranged the top boards as best you can, joint the edges straight. Glue the boards together, edge to edge. Let the glue dry thoroughly, then sand the joints clean and flush.

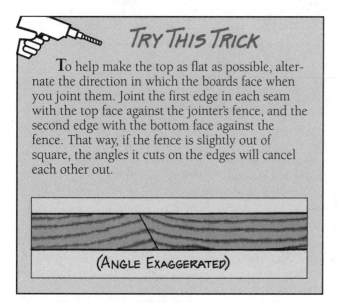

TRY THIS TRICK

To help make the top as flat as possible, alternate the direction in which the boards face when you joint them. Joint the first edge in each seam with the top face against the jointer's fence, and the second edge with the bottom face against the fence. That way, if the fence is slightly out of square, the angles it cuts on the edges will cancel each other out.

(ANGLE EXAGGERATED)

3 Cut the mortises and tenons. The legs and aprons are held together by pegged mortise-and-tenon joints. Rout ¼-inch-wide, ¹³⁄₁₆-inch-deep, 4-inch-long mortises in the faces of the legs, as shown in the *Leg Layout*. Cut tenons on the ends of the aprons to fit the mortises, as shown in the *Apron Layout* and the *Apron-to-Leg Joinery Detail*.

4 Taper the legs and the brace. The legs taper from 2 inches wide to 1 inch, as shown in the *Leg Layout*. Cut these tapers on the *inside* surfaces of the legs, using a band saw or a table saw. Joint the sawed

surfaces smooth. Also taper the ends of the brace, as shown in the *Brace Layout*.

5 Cut the notches in the aprons. Two opposite aprons must be notched to fit around the brace, as shown in the *Apron Layout*. Select which two aprons will be notched, lay out the notches, then cut them with a band saw or saber saw.

6 Drill screw pockets and shank holes. The tabletop is attached to the table with wood screws. Using a drill press, make screw pockets in the inside surfaces of the aprons, as shown in the *Top-to-Apron Joinery Detail*. Make four screw pockets in the notched aprons, and five in the remaining aprons. The screw pocket locations are not critical, but they should be fairly evenly spaced along the top edge of each apron.

Also drill ¼-inch-diameter countersunk shank holes in the brace, as shown in the *Brace Layout*, and in the screw pockets in the aprons. The holes in both the aprons and the brace will be larger than the shanks of the screws, letting the top expand and contract.

7 Assemble the table. Finish sand all the table parts. Glue the aprons and legs together. Allow the glue to dry, then peg the tenons in the mortises. Drill ⅜-inch-diameter, 1¼-inch-deep holes in the legs, through the mortises and the tenons, as shown in the *Side View* and the *End View*. Whittle each peg, making it more and more round toward one end. When you're finished, one end should be round and the other square, as shown in the *Peg Detail*. Coat each peg with glue, then drive the round ends into the holes in the legs. For more information on how to install the pegs, refer to *FIGURES 9-3 THROUGH 9-5* on page 112.

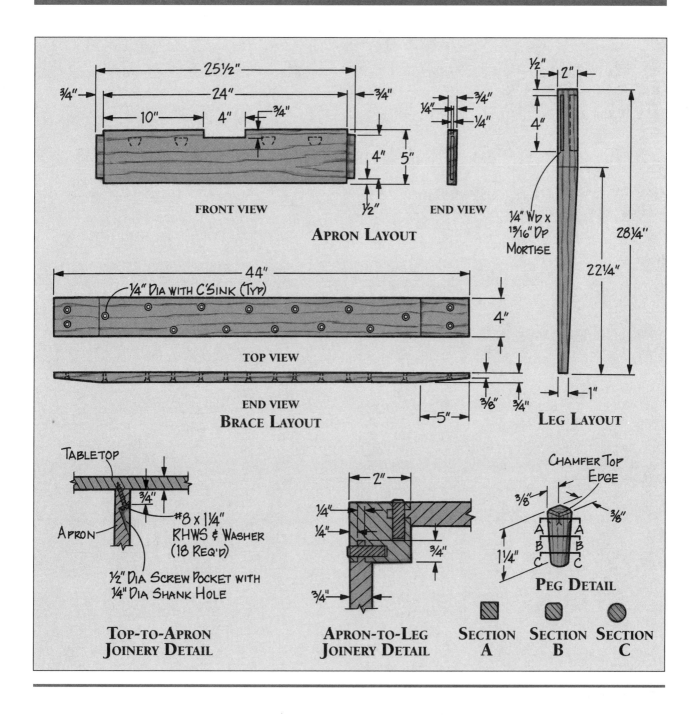

When the legs and aprons are assembled, rest the brace in the notched aprons. Place the top on the assembly and center it. Make sure the wood grain in the top is perpendicular to the brace. Fasten the top to the aprons with roundhead wood screws and washers, then attach the brace to the top with flathead wood screws.

8 **Finish the table.** Disassemble the top, brace, and leg assembly, setting the screws and washers aside. Do any necessary touch-up sanding, then apply a finish to all wooden surfaces. Be sure to put as many coats on the bottom of the tabletop as you do on the top. (If the bottom surface of the tabletop is left unfinished, or if the finish on the top and bottom are uneven, the bottom surface will absorb and release moisture at a different rate than the top surface. This, in turn, will cause the tabletop to warp.) When the finish is dry, rub it out and put the table back together.

INDEX

Note: Page references in *italic* indicate photographs or illustrations. **Boldface** references indicate charts or tables.

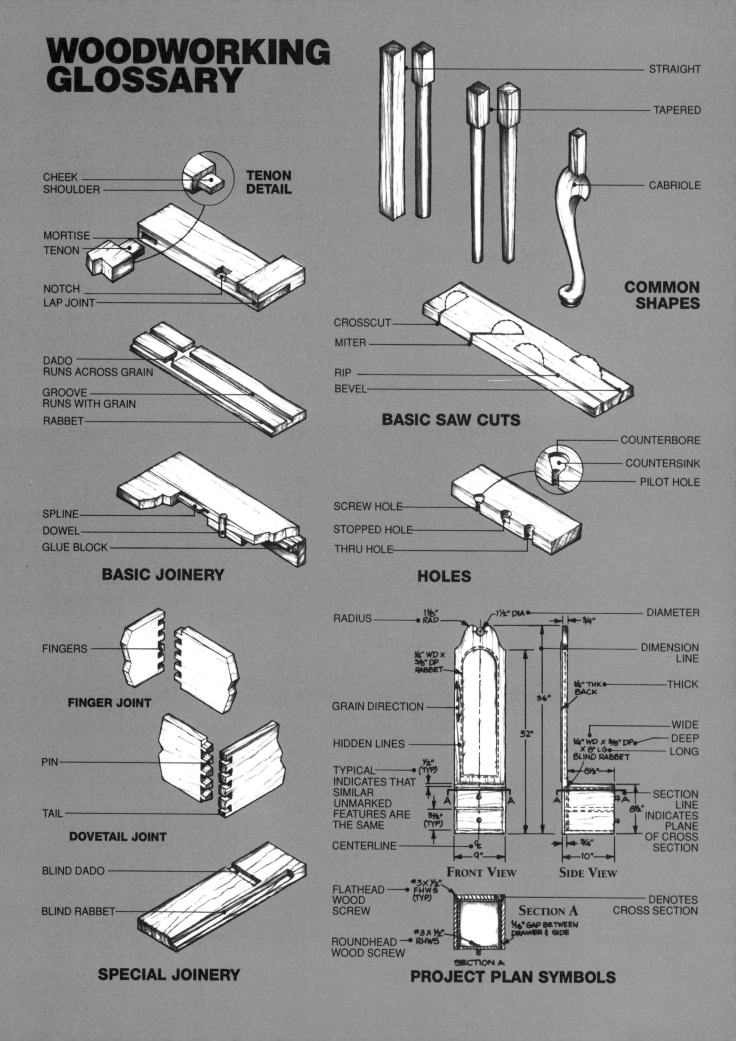

WOODWORKING GLOSSARY

TENON DETAIL
- CHEEK
- SHOULDER

- MORTISE
- TENON

- NOTCH
- LAP JOINT

- DADO RUNS ACROSS GRAIN
- GROOVE RUNS WITH GRAIN
- RABBET

BASIC JOINERY
- SPLINE
- DOWEL
- GLUE BLOCK

FINGER JOINT
- FINGERS

DOVETAIL JOINT
- PIN
- TAIL

SPECIAL JOINERY
- BLIND DADO
- BLIND RABBET

COMMON SHAPES
- STRAIGHT
- TAPERED
- CABRIOLE

BASIC SAW CUTS
- CROSSCUT
- MITER
- RIP
- BEVEL

HOLES
- COUNTERBORE
- COUNTERSINK
- PILOT HOLE
- SCREW HOLE
- STOPPED HOLE
- THRU HOLE

PROJECT PLAN SYMBOLS
- RADIUS — 1½" RAD
- 1½" DIA
- ¾"
- DIAMETER
- ¼" WD x ⅜" DP RABBET
- DIMENSION LINE
- ⅛" THK BACK — THICK
- 36"
- 32"
- GRAIN DIRECTION
- HIDDEN LINES
- ¼" WD X ⅜" DP X 8" LG BLIND RABBET
- WIDE
- DEEP
- LONG
- ½" (TYP)
- 8½"
- TYPICAL INDICATES THAT SIMILAR UNMARKED FEATURES ARE THE SAME
- 5½" (TYP)
- SECTION LINE INDICATES PLANE OF CROSS SECTION
- 8½"
- CENTERLINE
- 9"
- ¾"
- 10"
- **FRONT VIEW**
- **SIDE VIEW**
- FLATHEAD WOOD SCREW — #3 X ½" FHWS (TYP)
- **SECTION A**
- ¹⁄₁₆" GAP BETWEEN DRAWER & SIDE
- DENOTES CROSS SECTION
- ROUNDHEAD WOOD SCREW — #3 X ½" RHWS
- SECTION A